GOD'S PLAN FOR BUILDING A GOOD REPUTATION

GOD'S PLAN FOR
BUILDING A GOOD REPUTATION

GENE A. GETZ

While this book is intended for the reader's personal enjoyment and profit, it is also intended for group study. A Leader's Guide with Victor Multiuse Transparency Masters is available from your local bookstore or from the publisher.

VICTOR BOOKS®
A DIVISION OF SCRIPTURE PRESS PUBLICATIONS INC.
USA CANADA ENGLAND

Scripture quotations are from the *Holy Bible: New International Version*, © 1973, 1978, 1984 by the International Bible Society. Used by permission of Zondervan Bible Publishers.

Recommended Dewey Decimal Classification: 248.4
Suggested Subject Heading: CHRISTIAN LIFE

Library of Congress Catalog Card Number: 86-63161
ISBN: 0-89693-010-6

Renewal:
A Biblical Perspective

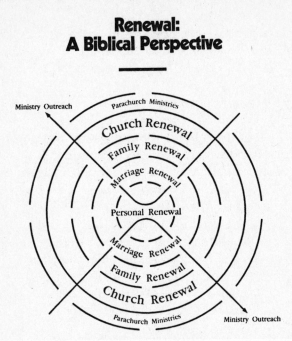

BIBLICAL RENEWAL

Renewal is the essence of dynamic Christianity and the basis on which Christians, both in a corporate or "body" sense and as individual believers, can determine the will of God. Paul made this clear when he wrote to the Roman Christians—"be transformed by the *renewing of your mind.* Then," he continued, "you will be able to test and approve what God's will is" (Rom. 12:2). Here Paul is talking about renewal in a corporate sense. In other words, Paul is asking these Christians as a *body* of believers to develop the mind of Christ through corporate renewal.

Personal renewal will not happen as God intended it unless it happens in the context of corporate renewal. On the other hand, corporate renewal will not happen as God intended without personal renewal. Both are necessary.

The larger circle above represents "church renewal." This

is the most comprehensive concept in the New Testament. However, every local church is made up of smaller, self-contained, but interrelated units. The *family* in Scripture emerges as the "church in miniature." In turn, the family is made up of an even smaller social unit—*marriage*. The third inner circle represents *personal* renewal, which is inseparably linked to all of the other basic units. Marriage is made up of two separate individuals who become one. The family is made up of parents and children who are also to reflect the mind of Christ. And the church is made up of not only individual Christians, but couples and families.

Though all of these social units are interrelated, biblical renewal can begin within any specific social unit. But wherever it begins—in the church, families, marriages, or individuals—the process immediately touches all the other social units. And one thing is certain! All that God says is consistent and harmonious. He does not have one set of principles for the Church and another set for the family, another for husbands and wives, and another for individual Christians. For example, the principles God outlines for local church elders, fathers, and husbands regarding their roles as leaders are interrelated and consistent. If they are not, we can be sure that we have not interpreted God's plan accurately.

The Biblical Renewal Series is an expanding library of books by Gene Getz designed to provide supportive help in moving toward renewal. Each of these books fits into one of the circles described above and will provoke thought, provide interaction and tangible steps toward growth. You will find a detailed listing of the Biblical Renewal Series titles on the following page.

Sharpening the Focus of the Church presents an overall perspective for Church Renewal. All of these books are available from your bookstore.

CONTENTS

HOW TO GET PEOPLE
TO LIKE AND RESPECT YOU

Is It Biblical?

A number of years ago, Dale Carnegie wrote a book entitled *How to Win Friends and Influence People.* It was filled with good practical advice based on good common sense. However, it had no biblical base, though most of what Carnegie suggested certainly reflected Christian values.

Is it proper for you as a Christian to want others to like and respect you? More specifically, is it right and proper to take action to actually cause that to happen?

The answer to these questions is a decided *yes!* In fact, if we're going to have any positive Christian influence on others—our mates, our children, our friends (both Christians and non-Christians), and those we work for or with, we *must* be liked and respected. And if we live as Christ told us to live, *most* people *will* like and respect us!

Understand, of course, that not everyone will like you even though they may respect you. And some people will neither like nor respect you. But God's plan is that most people will both like *and* respect us. There are exceptions, of course, simply because our Christian lifestyle may make some people uncomfortable, jealous, or even angry. But most people will like us and respect us—even if they disagree with us—if we follow God's formula. Peter, writing to Christians who were living among the worst sort of non-Christians, exhorted them to "live such good lives among the pagans that, though they accuse you of doing wrong, they may see your good deeds and glorify God on the day He visits us" (1 Peter 2:12).

"But," you say, "didn't Jesus teach that people may hate us because they hated Him?" (John 15:18) True! But remember that those who hated Christ, the apostles, and other New Testament Christians consisted primarily of a minority group—the Jewish religious leaders. The reason is that Jesus and His followers had become so popular that they were threatening these religious leaders. "If we let Him go on like this," they said on one occasion, "everyone will believe in Him" (John 11:48). Later it was because Christians in Jerusalem were "enjoying the favor of all the people" and because "the Lord added to their number daily those who were being saved" (Acts 2:47) that persecution broke out in that city—precipitated by the religious leaders who were losing their followers to Christianity (4:16-18; 5:12-18).

This is a book that outlines God's plan for building a good reputation—both among Christians and non-Christians. It is based on the qualities and characteristics Paul outlined for Titus for selecting spiritual leaders in the church (Titus 1:5-9). These characteristics will cause any person to be above reproach—to have a good reputation. A person who has a good reputation is a person who is liked and respected.

So . . . how can you get people to like and respect you? Become the kind of person described by Paul in his letter to Titus.

Gene A. Getz

CHAPTER ONE

Don't Be Overbearing

"He must be blameless—not overbearing." (Titus 1:7)

During my college years I had an overbearing roommate. That was not only my opinion. Though I came to know this person better than others (we lived together for over a year), all the Christians who worked in a close relationship with this young man came to this same conclusion. In fact, almost everyone felt a bit sorry for me!

Since I try to be tolerant and forgiving, I did my best to make this relationship work. But the more I gave in to his whims and wishes, and the more I tolerated his irritating behavior, the more he seemed to take advantage of the situation.

The day came when we were to part. As we sat together talking one evening, he "pushed me over the edge," and all the resentment and frustration I had allowed to build up within me came pouring out. I told him not only how I felt, but also how everyone else felt about his behavior.

Fortunately, God used that confrontation to get his attention. As I shared my frustration and deep feelings of hurt and anxiety, I literally wept. Though I certainly could have improved my method of communication that day, God used it nevertheless. Somehow my roommate saw beyond my frustration and anger to my personal concern for his welfare and his reputation as a Christian. Furthermore, he knew in his heart that I had patiently put up with a lot of self-oriented behavior on his part.

The results of that very emotional conversation were dramatic. Though he did not acknowledge at the time that what I had shared was true, his attitudes and actions changed. During the short time we were together after our confrontation, he immediately began to be more sensitive and "others oriented." I could tell that he was attempting to make some mid-course corrections in his life.

The great reward, however, came several years later. He acknowledged that everything I had said was true. He wanted me to know that even while I was pointing out those things in his life, he knew *then* it was true. But he couldn't bring himself to admit it. He wanted me to know that he had changed.

I share this not to put down my friend or to make myself look good (for I had my own share of immaturity—and still do), but I share it to illustrate that having an overbearing, self-pleasing, and self-oriented personality *does* affect one's reputation as a Christian. Generally speaking, people do not like and respect people with overbearing personalities. Though we may and should love them in spite of their attitudes and actions, it's difficult to have positive feelings toward these people. It is possible to *love* a person without *liking* that person. The *agape* love the Scriptures exhort us to have for one another calls for doing what is right no matter how we feel toward a person. God's plan, however, is that people both love and like us.

The Greek word *authadees,* which is translated "overbearing" in Titus 1:7, is used only twice in the New Testament. Peter used the word to graphically describe men "who follow the corrupt desire of the sinful nature and despise authority." They are "bold and arrogant [*authadees*]," Peter declares, and "are not afraid to slander celestial beings" (2 Peter 2:10). When we read on, it becomes clear that Peter is describing non-Christian people who "blaspheme in matters they do not understand. They are brute beasts, creatures of instinct, born only to be caught and destroyed, and like beasts they too will perish" (2 Peter 2:12).

"That's Not Me!"

This is the worst description of an overbearing person. But in using this word in his letter to Titus, Paul is teaching that Christians may also to some extent reflect this characteristic in their lives. Though believers, they have not yet begun to reflect Christ's spirit of humility and love. They are still arrogant, self-pleasing, and self-willed. They are still reflecting the "acts of the sinful nature" rather than "the fruit of the Spirit" (Gal. 5:19, 22).

Since the word *overbearing* can be used to describe a person whose arrogance and self-centeredness are blasphemous and horribly sinful, it is easy for Christians to rationalize and conclude that they don't display this characteristic in their lives. The fact is that we may actually be appalled at what Peter describes and yet still be overbearing, self-oriented, and self-pleasing Christians. We have simply sugarcoated our sinful behavior with regular church and Bible study attendance and the right religious language. In fact, we may have very strong biblical beliefs and yet be guilty of failure in this area of our lives. Even though our basic doctrines—what we believe about God, Jesus Christ, the Holy Spirit, and how to be saved—may be "above reproach," we may not have translated that truth as we should into practice.

Of course, there are various degrees of self-centeredness. Even very mature Christians have this tendency and fall into this trap. We'll find it easy to be self-pleasing and overbearing until Christ takes us home to heaven. But there is a point at which this kind of behavior breeds resentment, lack of respect, and lack of trust. If we persistently demonstrate this trait, people will not like and respect us. In fact, they'll avoid us altogether.

It is very difficult to confront a Christian with this trait. "Teachability" is not an overbearing person's long suit. Most people will not tell such a person how they feel. They are afraid, intimidated, and fear rejection and hurt. They may work very hard to please and be accepted by the overbearing one, but most of them are talking about him behind his back.

It is clear that this negative characteristic in our lives will not only affect our relationships with other believers in the church, but it will also affect our relationships in our families—our relationships with our spouses and our relationships with our children.

Marital Relationships

There is nothing more devastating to a marriage relationship than an overbearing, self-oriented spouse. Selfishness probably destroys more marriages than any other negative characteristic. At this level we discover the real truth about our mates—and ourselves.

How a person relates to Christians generally is not necessarily a true test of how that person will relate to his or her marriage partner. We may relate to others in the body of Christ in very unselfish ways, yet when faced with the challenge of relating to our mates, find ourselves gravitating toward selfish behavior. Twenty-four-hour, wall-to-wall relationships bring our weaknesses to the surface more quickly than casual, periodic relationships.

In some respects I found it easier to live for Christ when I was single than when I got married. Having to relate to my wife was far more demanding than having to relate to my friends, fellow Christians, and the larger Christian community. To love my Christian neighbors as Christ loved me is one thing; to love my wife as Christ loved the church is yet another thing. That's why I believe Paul emphasized this point in his letters to the Ephesians and Colossians (Eph. 5:25; Col. 3:19) after he had clearly stated that all Christians are to love one another as Christ loved them (Eph. 5:2; Col. 3:14). Paul knew that marriage puts far greater demands on our commitment to Christ. Not only am I made more aware of my own selfish tendencies, but I'm also faced with the challenge of living with my mate's weaknesses. The fact is, there is no perfect husband and no perfect wife. Unless we are really committed to practicing God's principles of love, our imperfections are likely to create alienation rather than mutual Christian growth and edification as God intended.

It's also interesting that after Paul exhorted all Christians to "submit to one another out of reverence for Christ," he immediately exhorted wives to submit to their husbands as to the Lord (Eph. 5:21-22). Again, it is often easier for wives to submit to others in the body of Christ than to submit to their own husbands. This, I believe, is one reason why Paul emphasized this point for wives—just as he emphasized "loving as Christ loved" for husbands. We have a natural tendency to violate these biblical principles.

Nowhere have I seen this natural tendency to be unsubmissive demonstrated more graphically than on the dozens of church ski trips I've organized and supervised. It happens when a husband tries to teach his wife how to ski. After many, many first-hand observations (and some personal experience, I might add), I learned to warn men not to attempt to teach their wives to ski. It is far safer and much more productive for a husband to pay a ski instructor for the lessons. Both will enjoy the whole ski trip much more— because if a husband gets his wife angry on the first day on the slopes, she may be angry all week. This is particularly true when she rejects her husband's efforts and he, in turn, gets mad and starts yelling instructions. From that point forward it's all downhill.

I must quickly add that I've seen some notable exceptions. A woman who is teachable under these circumstances has really passed the test, as has her husband, for it takes a great deal of mutual trust and love to be able to practice Christlike attitudes and actions.

Let me add a special word of warning to husbands. Though both spouses can be guilty of being overbearing and selfish (it lies just below the surface for most of us), the man can perhaps more easily be guilty of developing this quality. There are several reasons. First, by God's design the man is to be the leader in the home. Because of his sinful nature, even as a Christian, a man's natural tendency is to abuse this position. Second, a husband's ego is easily threatened (one of a man's greatest weaknesses), which can very quickly lead to selfish reactions. Third, a man tends to operate more at the rational level than the feeling level, and he often does not understand how his overbearing approach to leadership is affecting his wife. When she tries to tell him how she feels, rather than listening, he gives her ten reasons why she shouldn't feel that way!

If the truth be known, a man often responds to his wife with logic because he is threatened by her negative feelings. He is not only trying to prove to her that she shouldn't feel the way she does, but he is also trying to prove to himself that he is not to blame for her feelings.

Good reputations (being liked and respected) really begin with our relationships with our spouses. That's the true test. The great challenge for husbands and wives is to demonstrate unselfish, Christlike behavior.

Parent-Child Relationships

The ability to be humble and kind to others is tested even further in our relationships with our children. An overbearing father or mother can devastate and discourage children. Though this is true for both parents, it's particularly applicable to fathers. That is why Paul wrote, "Fathers, do not exasperate your children; instead bring them up in the training and instruction of the Lord" (Eph. 6:4). In his letter to the Colossians he stated it even more specifically: "Fathers, do not embitter your children, or they will become discouraged" (Col. 3:21).

An overbearing, insensitive parent can create unusual anger and resentment in children. This should not surprise us, since this kind of behavior creates anger and resentment in adults. I'm quite amazed at how often we expect children to tolerate adult weaknesses and our own immature behavior to a greater degree than we tolerate the same kind of behavior in ourselves or in other adults. Yet a child is far less capable of handling these problems intellectually and emotionally than we are simply because of his chronological immaturity.

Have you found yourself doing that to your children? I know I have. And what is more significant, I find that I often become most frustrated with my children's weaknesses when they mirror the weaknesses I find in myself.

In all these relationships, being overbearing will contribute to a bad reputation. We need to guard against this characteristic in our lives if we want to pursue God's plan for getting others to like and respect us.

CHAPTER TWO

Control Your Temper

"He must be ... not quick-tempered." (Titus 1:7)

Not all anger is wrong. Neither do all kinds of anger mean a person is "quick-tempered." In fact it is impossible to live without feeling anger; it is a normal human emotion. To deny this reality in ourselves and others can lead to some serious psychological and spiritual—and even physical—problems. It's possible to experience and express anger without sinning. Jesus Christ, the perfect Son of God, demonstrated this when He drove the moneychangers from the temple. Seeing them exploiting others—in the very house of God—He overturned their tables and scattered their money all over the courtyard. He even made a whip out of cords and drove the sheep and cattle out of the temple area (John 2:13-17).

Note that it doesn't say He used the whip on the people—though they deserved it. Note also that His anger was based on the fact that these people were taking advantage of people who had come to offer sacrifices to God. It was the ultimate in exploitation of a sacred place and a sacred event.

Paul also spoke about anger and sin. Writing to the Ephesians, he said, "In your anger do not sin" (Eph. 4:26). Paul was saying that when we get angry—and we all do—we should not sin. This leads us to a very basic question.

When Does Anger Become Sinful?

Paul's maturity profile in his letter to Titus answers this question at least partially.

● Anger becomes sinful when it results in "quick-tempered" behavior.

This is not some great profound truth. All of us understand what Paul is talking about. The word Paul uses in Titus 1:7 literally means "passionate." A quick-tempered person "flies off the handle," "loses his cool," and usually says and does things that hurt and offend others.

The word also implies *persistent* behavior. Paul is not talking about isolated and periodic circumstances that push us over the edge. A quick-tempered person consistently and persistently loses his temper.

● Anger becomes sinful when it hurts people physically.

This kind of behavior correlates with another negative characteristic listed by Paul in the same text. A Christian who is violent is certainly immature. The concept here actually means to be a "striker"—to hurt people through physical force.

Because this is becoming such a problem in our society, we have devoted an entire chapter to dealing with the subject. More than many Christians realize, violence in our society is affecting the way Christians act and respond to one another.

● Anger becomes sinful when it persists and results in bitterness.

Paul spoke directly to this issue when he wrote, "In your anger do not sin." Elaborating on what he meant, he stated— "Do not let the sun go down while you are still angry, and do not give the devil a foothold" (Eph. 4:26-27).

All of us need a cooling-off period when we get angry. It is virtually impossible to suddenly flip a switch and dissipate these feelings. But time is a friend. It gives us an opportunity to understand what has happened and to become more objective.

I have personally found it very helpful to not write letters or make telephone calls when I'm angry. If I do write a letter, I always hold it for at least twenty-four hours, reread it, and often tear it up. I've also found it beneficial not to respond verbally to a person or situation when my feelings are unusually intense. If I do, I'll usually say things I'm sorry for.

There is a fine line here, for at times we should respond immediately. It's the right time to deal with the problem. But in doing so—and we all know ourselves—we should be able to respond maturely and in a nonvindictive and nondefensive way. It is not wrong to share our feelings of anger, but in sharing these feelings we should not attack the other person. For example, a person might say, "I'm feeling very angry right now. I feel threatened and hurt and misunderstood—though I'm sure I don't understand all the factors involved." We can be sure that this is always true even though we may not feel it is. There are always factors we don't understand. It is much different to shout, "I'm angry. Why do you always pick on me? What's the beef? What's your problem? Why are you so insensitive? Can't you see what you're doing to me and everyone else?"

Regarding misunderstanding, several weeks before I wrote this chapter, I sensed a strain in my relationship with my wife. Frankly, I couldn't understand what was happening to cause the problem. At first I thought it was just one of those moments in the stream of life we all experience, and it would pass. But it didn't. We didn't argue; it was just something I felt.

Finally, I awakened one morning and broached the subject with my wife, trying to be teachable myself. I was amazed at what I heard. She was interpreting certain things in my attitudes and actions that had precipitated her responses. I had in turn responded that way because of some things she had said—which I had totally misunderstood. We had had a breakdown in communication that led to our mutual misinterpretation. Fifteen minutes of honestly and openly sharing thoughts and feelings in a nonjudgmental and nondefensive way changed our perceptions of the problem—and resolved it. I was amazed at how two people can live together for over thirty years and so totally misunderstand each other's thoughts and feelings.

To allow these situations to persist can lead to bitterness and increasingly aggressive actions. We are allowing the sun to go down while we're still angry. We're giving the devil a foothold in our lives. I don't believe Paul is speaking literally here in terms of a twenty-four hour day. It certainly is a good idea to settle issues before the day ends—providing that's possible. But some problems erupt as the sun is going down.

The point Paul is making is that we need some time to think, reflect, and cool off, but we should not allow anger to persist. If we do, it will become sinful. We'll do things and say things that are wrong.

● Anger becomes sinful when we hurt people emotionally and spiritually.

We must remember that it is also possible to hurt people with words. In fact, verbal abuse can be more devastating than physical abuse. I remember one occasion when I was working on one of my weekly messages while at the same time enjoying a hamburger at McDonald's. A young mother was there with two of her children. Suddenly she began to verbally and mercilessly attack her young son. He must have been about five or six years old. I don't know what he did to irritate her (maybe he spilled something), but I'll never forget his response to her angry outburst. I could see him withdraw into a physical stance reflecting horrible humiliation. He never said a word, nor did he cry. He simply withered like a green plant sprayed with powerful poison.

But the barrage didn't stop with a volley of verbal abuse inside the restaurant. Minutes later they left, crossed the parking lot to her car, and before getting in, she cut loose again. This time she came at him with a pointed finger and strong language. She must have verbally abused him for two minutes—as the little guy turned his head away trying to escape this psychological beating. You might guess what she said when he looked away. "Turn and look at me!" she shouted. I clearly remember his efforts as he tried to raise his eyes and look into her ugly countenance. (I'm showing my own emotions now.)

By that time I *was* becoming angry. In fact, I can feel the same emotions as I recount the story. I wanted to grab this woman and shake her and shout a few choice words myself. Obviously, I didn't know all the factors involved. But one thing I was sure of. Here was an angry, frustrated woman—and that little guy was the scapegoat. No matter what he did (and it couldn't have been much), the mother's behavior reflected a very quick-tempered and verbally violent woman.

Don't misunderstand. I'm not saying children do not need discipline. But we should avoid publicly embarrassing our children. And we should not displace our anger on them—no matter what their misdemeanors.

● Anger becomes sinful when we become vengeful.

It is a natural tendency to want to hurt those who hurt us—to get even. But that, God says, is not our right or our responsibility. Paul wrote, "Do not repay anyone evil for evil. . . . Do not take revenge, my friends, but leave room for God's wrath, for it is written: 'It is mine to avenge, I will repay,' says the Lord." It is God's will for all of us to "overcome evil with good" rather than to "be overcome with evil" (Rom. 12:17, 19, 21).

Again, we must understand that to share our feelings of anger and frustration in a straightforward and nonjudgmental way is not taking vengeance. Vengeance means getting even and punishing other people for their actions toward us. That's God's prerogative. Our responsibility is to forgive them and to attempt to work through the problem. Sometimes people will respond. On occasions they will not respond. But if we have done our part, then we can proceed with a free conscience.

What Causes Sinful Anger?

There are several reasons why we allow angry feelings to lead to sinful actions.

● We are made in God's image.

God is a God of love and a God of anger. And we are made in His image. Therefore we have a unique capacity for both of these emotions and the reactions they cause. When Adam and Eve plunged the whole world into sin, our problem became tremendously complicated. Very quickly angry feelings could lead to sinful actions. The point we must understand, however, is that anger is a God-created capacity that reflects His image. It should not surprise us that we experience this emotion so easily and so consistently. In view of the sin problem we all face, it should not surprise us that we have so much trouble with this emotion.

● We may have been exposed to bad models.

Angry people nurture anger in others. Thus Solomon wrote, "Do not make friends with a hot-tempered man, do not associate with one easily angered, or you may learn his ways and get yourself ensnared" (Prov. 22:24-25). This is an especially serious problem when the bad model is a child's parent. Children cannot suddenly remove themselves from a bad home environment. The important lesson here focuses on us who are parents. Our children need, not perfect models, but good models. They need to be able to watch people who demonstrate how to handle anger in mature ways.

Remember too that children can understand anger. If we

totally hide our own anger from them, they may grow up thinking that it is wrong to have angry feelings. This can lead to real guilt feelings on their part.

I remember one time when my son was in his most active period of life. He must have been about eight or nine. We were sitting at the dinner table. He had his spoon in his iced tea and was clinking it against the side of the glass.

Frankly, it irritated me. I had had a pretty rough day and just the sound of the clinking glass disturbed me. So I asked him to stop. And he did—for a few seconds. Then he began to clink again.

And once again I asked him to stop—this time with a little more intensity in my voice. Again he cooperated—for a few seconds. The third time it happened, I turned to him, asked him to look me straight in the eye, and said with more intensity than ever, "Kenton, I've asked you to stop two times already. Now please obey. That noise makes me angry!"

My son looked at me somewhat startled. Then with a very calm spirit, he said, "Oh, OK, Dad! I understand." This time he really understood and stopped. He needed to hear me share my anger in a direct, but nonabusive way. *That* he understood.

● We can easily develop bad habits.

Angry outbursts can become a habit. We learn that we can sometimes manipulate others with this approach to problems. We've simply developed a bad habit—a way of responding.

Or we may have concluded from past experiences that this is the normal way to behave. It becomes so much a part of our behavior that it is as natural as breathing. Unfortunately, we are responding in an inappropriate way because that is the way we've learned to respond.

● We may have been mistreated.

This is the most difficult problem to correct and overcome. Unfortunately, children are most often the victims—

although more and more the battered spouse syndrome is emerging. Most women who become victims are battered physically. Most men who are victims are battered psychologically.

From a Christian point of view, the most applicable point is to make sure we are not guilty of abuse. Certainly, if we know it's happening to others, we should do all we can to help, realizing that it is not always the easiest problem to resolve.

One of my close friends looked out of his window one evening in the Chicago area. A man was in the middle of the street beating his wife. Being a good, concerned citizen, my friend went out into the street and tried to break up the fight. Unexpectedly, when he pulled the man off the woman, she immediately turned on my friend and began to attack him. The response went something like this: "This is none of your affair. If my husband wants to beat me up, that's his business—not yours!"

A strange response indeed! But unfortunately our efforts are not always appreciated by those who are victims.

● We may sin in our anger out of insecurity.

Strange as it may seem, a sense of insecurity causes angry outbursts more than any other psychological factor. Threatened people lose their cool very quickly. We've all experienced that tendency because all of us have felt threatened on occasion.

I remember when I was a young teacher at Moody Bible Institute. I had a student in one of my classes who was constantly irritating me. He was older than I was, which complicated matters. After enduring his verbal and nonverbal barbs for several weeks, one day I had had enough. I simply closed my notebook and walked out, leaving the class in the middle of the hour.

To be perfectly honest, I felt threatened by this man's behavior, and it made me very angry. I couldn't handle the situation any longer, so I removed myself. Needless to say, I was extremely embarrassed the next time I met the class. Though I had acted immaturely, most of my students understood the situation and were quite forgiving. I hope I had the grace to apologize for my behavior, though frankly I can't remember.

It's interesting that I later found out why this man was badgering me. Unknown to me, he was attracted to the woman I was dating, who later became my wife. He felt I had stolen her away from him. After Elaine and I were married, he came and apologized for what he had done and sought my forgiveness. It was then I learned the cause of his behavior. But it is still true that I was not mature enough emotionally to handle that classroom situation, and the basis of my actions and reactions was threat.

Overcoming Sinful Anger
Learning to control anger takes understanding and insight. This truth is clear in the Proverbs.
- "He who is slow to anger has great understanding" (Prov. 14:29, NASB).
- "He who restrains his words has knowledge, and he who has a cool spirit is a man of understanding" (17:27, NASB).
- "A man's discretion makes him slow to anger" (19:11, NASB).

The more we understand the circumstances that cause anger in ourselves and others, the more we will be able to control that anger and handle it in ourselves and others. We need mature perception.

For example, if insecurity is at the root of many of our angry outbursts, we need to understand that and be on guard against it. I have found that when I'm verbally attacked by someone, asking myself the question, *Why is this person responding this way?* helps me accept the abuse without responding in like manner. This has been particularly true for me in public situations where I have been attacked in a classroom or in a seminar. Usually, if I can perceive the situation correctly, I can see that I have threatened that person in some way, or that he or she has some serious problems. The natural tendency, of course, is to counter-attack, particularly if you are in a position of authority. But obviously, that is not a mature response.

I remember the first time I spoke in Hong Kong. It was in one of the first sessions of a pastors' conference. Toward the end of the session, a man walked in and listened to a few statements that I made—out of context. He then stood up and began to verbally attack me. Since he was from Great Britain, he spoke English. He claimed to be a prophet of God and he believed he was called there to reveal that I was a *false* prophet. Since this was my first time in a Chinese culture, and since I was speaking through an interpreter, I found myself in a rather difficult situation. Fortunately, God gave me grace to respond with kindness. I listened and then suggested that we get together following the meeting to talk about his concerns. In that instance a gentle answer turned away wrath (Prov. 15:1).

That was not my only encounter with that man during the time I was in Hong Kong. We did meet, but it turned out not to be very productive. I found out later from another pastor that this man was indeed very disturbed.

Understanding, therefore, is not always easy. There are certain cases where individuals have repressed anger in themselves to the point that they do not really understand why they respond the way they do. One of the saddest situations I can recall involves a grown woman who served as a full-time missionary. She never married until she met another Christian leader whose wife had died. A short time after she married, she began to experience incredible de-pression. She didn't understand the problem; it was a new experience.

Through professional help she remembered that she had been sexually abused by her father (and by other men) as a little child. The experience was so painful that she had repressed all of the anger and negative emotions that accompanied that experience. She could not remember the events until they were revealed in therapy. It was then that she could begin to understand and deal with her anger and depression.

This is an unusual circumstance, but I share it to indicate that there are cases in which a person has been hurt so badly that normal perception and understanding is virtually impossible. I wish there were simple answers to these problems. There are not. Bringing this kind of problem to the surface sometimes makes the problem worse, at least for a time. That is why it calls for an experienced therapist. This kind of problem must be handled very carefully. Fortunately, most of our problems are not this complex.

There are some who teach that just expressing anger releases it and solves the problem. This is not necessarily true. In fact, studies show that it can intensify anger and generate more. Without proper understanding, insight, and the ability to control anger in biblical ways, the problem can go unsolved or get worse.

Preventive Maintenance

In my book *The Measure of a Man*, I suggest some ideas for keeping our emotions under control (pp. 110-111). Let me repeat them here.

1. Stay in tune spiritually. Avoid getting out of fellowship with God. Keep your prayer life in order and listen to the voice of God as He speaks through the Scriptures.

2. Avoid having to face difficult and tense situations when you are physically or emotionally drained.

3. Engage in a regular program of physical exercise, especially if you work under pressure and consistent tension.

Mothers who are cooped up all day with small children are no exception. They are particularly vulnerable.

4. If you become angry and upset over a situation and you are unable to shake the problem, learn to express your feelings in an objective and straightforward manner. Don't brood! Communicate.

5. Learn to back away from an aggravating situation and look at it objectively. Why did it happen? What problems may the other person involved be facing? Ask yourself what you can do to help become a part of the solution rather than a part of the problem.

6. Memorize James 1:19-20. If anger is a problem in your life, meditate on these verses every morning before you begin your day's activities. Then ask God to help you put this truth into practice: "My dear brothers, take note of this: Everyone should be quick to listen, slow to speak and slow to become angry, for man's anger does not bring about the righteous life that God desires" (James 1:19-20).

As you bring your quick temper under control, you will find yourself on the way to a good reputation.

CHAPTER THREE

Don't Overindulge in Anything

"He must be . . . not given to much wine." (Titus 1:7)

Several years ago I received a letter in the mail from an irate mother on the West Coast. She was having some very serious problems with her teenage son. He was drinking. Someone recommended that she give him a copy of my book *The Measure of a Man*, which has a chapter on each of the twenty qualities of maturity that Paul listed in his letters to Titus and Timothy. She, of course, decided to read the book herself before giving it to her son, which is commendable. However, when she got to Chapter 9, entitled "Not Addicted to Wine," she became very angry, tore up the book, and threw it in the trash. In her letter she accused me of false teaching and condemned me for perverting the Word of God and leading people astray.

Evidently she had read the first paragraph and decided I was a heretic. Let me share that paragraph and you'll understand *why* she was so upset.

If Paul were living today in our twentieth-century Western culture, would he condone drinking alcoholic beverages? Not necessarily, as will be shown later. But the issue before us in 1 Timothy and Titus is *not* total abstinence from any form of alcoholic beverage. The basic word *paroinos* used in these verses literally means a man who "sits too long at his wine." In other words, he *overdrinks*, and consequently is brought into bondage and loses control of his senses. (p. 84)

What Does the Bible Teach about Drinking Alcoholic Beverages?

The Bible does not teach against drinking alcoholic beverages per se. Don't misunderstand! Total abstinence, particularly in our culture, is an excellent goal for every Christian. *Before you complete this chapter, I frankly trust you'll consider making total abstinence your goal*—particularly in certain situations. But we cannot demonstrate that New Testament Christians did not drink alcoholic beverages. Jesus Christ Himself—and this might shock some people—probably both made and drank wine that had alcoholic content. John records that Jesus miraculously changed water into "choice wine" (John 2:10)—the same words that are used for fermented wine in other places in the New Testament (Mark 2:22; Eph. 5:18). Furthermore, Jesus Himself stated of His accusers: "For John [the Baptist] came neither eating nor drinking, and they say, 'He has a demon.' The Son of Man came eating and drinking, and they say, 'Here is a glutton and a drunkard, a friend of tax collectors and sinners'" (Matt. 11:18-19).

Here, in the context, the term "drinking" definitely seems to refer to alcoholic beverages. This is why Jesus' critics called Him a "drunkard"—which, of course, He wasn't. For Jesus, to drink wine and to be a drunkard are two different things.

That Jesus drank wine at least on occasions is further suggested by the very contrast between Himself and John the Baptist in this verse. John did not come eating and drinking; Jesus did both. This contrast is highlighted by the fact that

John was "never to take wine or other fermented drink" (Luke 1:15)—no doubt to set him apart in a unique way as a forerunner of the Lord. But this restriction was not placed on other followers of Christ, and Christ did not place this restriction on Himself.

This was also true of other spiritual leaders which is clear in Paul's letter to Titus. Local church elders "must be blameless—not overbearing, not quick-tempered, not given to much wine" (Titus 1:7, see also 1 Tim. 3:3, 8). Another translation reads, "not addicted to wine" (Titus 1:7, NASB). Paul was not saying they could not partake of wine; rather he was teaching that they should not be addicted to it, losing control of mind and body.

This leads us to what the Bible does teach about drinking alcoholic beverages.

The Bible clearly teaches against drunkenness. This is true in both the Old and New Testaments. In Proverbs we read, "Do not join those who drink too much wine or gorge themselves on meat, for drunkards and gluttons become poor, and drowsiness clothes them in rags" (Prov. 23:20-21).

Later in the same chapter we discover a series of questions: "Who has woe? Who has sorrow? Who has strife? Who has complaints? Who has needless bruises? Who has bloodshot eyes?" (Prov. 23:29) Following this series of very specific questions, we find the answer to all of them: "Those who linger over wine, who go to sample bowls of mixed wine" (23:30).

We then find a serious warning.

Do not gaze at wine when it is red,
    when it sparkles in the cup,
    when it goes down smoothly!
In the end it bites like a snake
    and poisons like a viper.

Your eyes will see strange sights
and your mind imagine confusing things.
(Prov. 23:31-33)

New Testament writers are just as clear in their teaching against overdrinking leading to drunkenness. Paul wrote to the Ephesians, "Do not get drunk on wine, which leads to debauchery. Instead, be filled with the Spirit" (Eph. 5:18).

In addition, the wine of New Testament days was not like our wine today. This is not totally clear from the biblical text as such. But it is very clear from other reliable sources. Dr. Norman Geisler, in his excellent booklet entitled *To Drink or Not to Drink* (Quest Publications, p. 16) summarized Robert H. Stine's excellent article, "Wine Drinking in New Testament Times" (*Christianity Today*, June 20, 1975, pp. 9-11). Geisler states,

> Stine researched wine drinking in the ancient world, in Jewish sources and in the Bible. He pointed out that wine in Homer's day was 20 parts water and one part wine (Odyssey 9.208.9). Pliny referred to wine as eight parts water and one part wine (Natural History, 14.6.54). According to Aristophanes, it was stronger, three parts water and two parts wine. Other classical Greek writers spoke of other mixtures. . . . The average was about three or four parts of water to one part of wine.

Geisler points out, "Wine today has a much higher level of alcohol than wine in the New Testament. In fact, in New Testament times one would need to drink 22 glasses of wine in order to consume the same amount of alcohol in two martinis today!" Again quoting Stine, Geisler concludes, "In other words, it is possible to become intoxicated with wine mixed with three parts of water, but one's drinking would probably affect the bladder long before the mind" (p. 17).

In view of this historical evidence, we must be careful not to equate wine drinking in today's world with wine drinking in the New Testament culture. There is definitely a difference. What we drink today would be classified in the Bible as strong drink—wine that is "red" and that "sparkles in the cup" (Prov. 23:31).

When Is Drinking Alcoholic Beverages Unwise or Sinful?

We've already noted that *overdrinking and overindulgence is wrong*. It is definitely a sin. Paul underscores this point in his letter to the Corinthians.

> Do you not know that the wicked will not inherit the kingdom of God? Do not be deceived: Neither the sexually immoral nor idolators nor adulterers nor male prostitutes nor homosexual offenders nor thieves nor the greedy nor drunkards nor slanderers nor swindlers will inherit the kingdom of God. And that is what some of you were. But you were washed, you were sanctified, you were justified in the name of the Lord Jesus Christ and by the Spirit of our God. (1 Cor. 6:9-11)

Drinking alcoholic beverages is also wrong *when we become addicted.* Paul wrote, " 'Everything is lawful for me'—but not everything is beneficial. 'Everything is permissible for me'—but I will not be mastered by anything" (1 Cor. 6:12).

There are some people who indulge in drinking and violate the will of God. But there are those people who indulge and also become addicted. They are overpowered by alcohol. They *consistently* overindulge. Today we classify these people as alcoholics.

Anyone who knows statistics is aware that America is an alcoholic society. According to the National Council on Alcoholism, a 1985 report revealed that 18.3 million adults in the United States are considered "heavy" drinkers. A "heavy drinker" consumes more than fourteen drinks per week. Of this 18.3 million, 12.1 million show one or more symptoms of alcoholism. In 1986, the Richardson Independent School District (in the Dallas area) reported that 80,000 Texan adolescents were alcoholics.

There is, of course, a difference of opinion among Christians regarding alcoholism. Some classify it as a sin; others as a disease. My personal opinion is that it is both. Alcoholism and overindulgence go together. There is evidence that this affliction is a sickness. But many other sinful actions, including homosexuality, rape, addiction to pornography, prostitution, various forms of crime (including stealing and lying and even murder) may have their roots in psychological problems or sicknesses. This does not disqualify these actions from being regarded as sinful. They are wrong. Unless they are recognized as "acts of the sinful nature" as well as acts caused by other factors in the personality, these problems will not be dealt with properly. People too easily rationalize their sinful behavior.

It is also true that alcoholics need understanding. They do not need our condemnation. Most already feel condemned. Often their self-image is at zero. They need to experience God's forgiveness in Jesus Christ. But they must also recognize that they are accountable for their actions—before both God and man.

Drinking is wrong *when it causes others to sin.* The Bible teaches that we should not cause others to stumble and fall into sin. Paul wrote to the Romans, "It is better not to eat meat or drink wine or to do anything else that will cause your brother to fall" (Rom. 14:21).

This has particular application to parents. The National Council on Alcoholism has discovered that children of alcoholics run a risk of becoming alcoholics themselves four times greater than that of children of nonalcoholics. True, we can engage in the age-old argument regarding what causes these kinds of problems—heredity or the environment. Both are involved. There are people (some say one in five) who are born with a propensity toward alcoholism, but it is still true that modeling plays a great part in causing these people to actually start drinking. Thus with a propensity to become addicted, these children are simply moved in that direction by a bad example. Of course, it is not just the drinking that leads these children astray, for there are also many emotional and spiritual problems created by an alcoholic parent.

The issue is far greater than children with a natural inclination to alcoholism—either psychologically or physically or both. What our children see can become a norm for them. Even though we may be "moderate drinkers," our children live in an alcoholic society. They have incredible peer pressures. It takes a very well-adjusted adolescent to refuse to indulge with his or her friends. Social acceptance is a tremendous force, and even children with good parental models can be led astray.

Within a period of two weeks two men in our church approached me regarding drinking alcoholic beverages. Both are growing Christians who desire to do the will of God. But the factor that triggered their concern about their actions was their young children. Looking at the problems in our society and what we know about alcoholism they were concerned about the example they might set for their children. Was it worth the risk—even though drinking may not be sin for them? Would their "freedom in Christ" eventually cause one of their children to fall? They both came to the conclusion as we discussed the matter that it was not worth the risk. One decided on total abstinence. The other decided on abstinence in front of the children. Both made decisions based on principles of Scripture.

Using alcohol is wrong *when we hurt ourselves or others.* The Bible clearly teaches that the bodies of Christians are temples of the Holy Spirit. He dwells within us. Therefore we are not to harm ourselves. We are not our own. We are bought at a price! "Therefore," Paul concludes, "honor God with your body" (1 Cor. 6:20).

Research points to the fact that overindulging does harm our bodies and affects our minds. One of the men who came to me mentioned a second reason why he wanted to quit drinking. After a hard day in the office, it did quiet his spirit and soothe his nerves to have several drinks. But he went on to point out that it put him in a state of lethargy. He had no desire to do anything but sit and watch TV or sleep. When his children and wife needed his attention, he lacked motivation to respond—which he noticed was directly related to his consumption of alcohol.

Drinking has even greater negative effects in our culture. Listen to these sobering facts.

1. Alcohol is the number 3 public health problem in the United States.

2. Alcohol is the number 1 cause of death among young people (ages 15–24).

3. Alcohol causes problems in more than one-third of all American families.

4. About 200,000 Americans are killed each year in alcohol-related incidents. This is nearly four times as many Americans as were killed in the entire Vietnam war.

5. One-half of all traffic accidents involve alcohol.

6. Drinking drivers are three to four times more likely to cause an accident than nondrinkers.

7. Alcohol is the third greatest cause of birth defects.

8. A high percentage of wife and child abuse cases result from alcohol.

9. There is a high correlation between alcoholic consumption and crimes such as suicide, homicide, rape, assault, and robbery.

These facts speak for themselves. Every Christian should

consider not only what the Bible teaches, but what research has revealed regarding drinking in our culture. Is it worth the risk to become part of the statistics that state that seven out of ten Americans use alcohol as a beverage?

Don't Overindulge in Anything

You'll notice how often eating and drinking are mentioned together in the Bible. There are Christians who overeat with regularity and yet would never touch a drop of alcohol. In fact, some of the Christians who are the most vociferous in their fight against drinking are consistently overweight. It's usually not because of glandular problems. It is a problem of self-discipline. At this point, these words of Jesus are applicable:

> Why do you look at the speck of sawdust in your brother's eye and pay no attention to the plank in your own eye? How can you say to your brother, "Let me take the speck out of your eye," when all the time there is a plank in your own eye? You hypocrite, first take the plank out of your own eye, and then you will see clearly to remove the speck from your brother's eye. (Matt. 7:3-5)

Tobacco Too!

I've never preached a sermon against smoking, though I've not smoked during my adolescent and adult life. Ironically I smoked more as a child, when two of my cousins taught me at age four and five to pick up cigarette butts along the highway. In retrospect I thank God that my parents moved when I was six and I got away from this negative influence. Otherwise, I probably would have become addicted to cigarettes, along with millions of other Americans.

The fact is that we cannot deny the harmful effects of smoking on our bodies. The statistics are piling up. Listen to these observations from the American Lung Association:

1. Cigarette smoking is the major cause of emphysema, chronic bronchitis, lung cancer, and heart disease.

2. Pregnant women who smoke have more spontaneous abortions, premature births, and low-weight births than women who do not smoke.

3. Nearly one million teenagers take up smoking every year. (There are now more girls smoking than boys.)

4. Over 350,000 people die yearly from diseases associated with smoking.

5. One-third of the deaths from heart disease are caused by smoking.

6. If people never smoked, 85 percent of lung cancer deaths would be avoided.

The Department of Health, Education and Welfare in 1979 estimated annual productivity losses from smoking at $71 billion. The National Center for Health Statistics calculated that 87 million work days are lost per year because of health problems related to smoking. Another study set the economic cost of smoking in the workplace in January 1980 at $47.5 billion, of which $11 billion was excess medical care for smokers. Another $36.5 billion in indirect costs was attributed to loss in the GNP from absenteeism, early retirement, and untimely deaths.

Along this same line, I was interested in an article in *The Denver Post* dated March 12, 1986 that treated the government's efforts at banning cigarette sales at military commissaries. A military study concluded that smoking cost the Pentagon hundreds of millions of dollars for health care. In fiscal year 1984 alone, "smoking-related costs" totalled at least $209.9 million.

Drugs

While flying back from Denver one evening, I was seated by a man who was reading *Newsweek* magazine. The feature article dealt with "Kids and Cocaine" (March 17, 1986, pp.

58–65). Since I was working on this chapter, I was particularly interested in what he was reading and told him why. When he was finished, he shared the magazine with me, which opened up a very interesting discussion between us after I had read it too. He was a Jew and I was a Christian.

Frankly, we were both shocked at what we read. "As thousands of teens have already learned to their families' infinite sorrow," the author states, "coke is *it* in the 1980s—the most glamorous, seductive, destructive, dangerous drug on the supersaturated national black market." The article goes on to point out that "cocaine abuse is the fastest-growing drug problem in America for adults and school-age children alike. The plain fact is that coke is widely available at low prices—within the financial reach of the young. And the plain fact is that coke is now being sold and used in an especially destructive new form. The new coke goes by many names on the street, but it is usually called 'crack' or 'rock.' It is smoked, not snorted, and the resulting intoxication is far more intense than that of snorted cocaine—much quicker, much more euphoric and much, much more addictive."

We must face the fact, particularly as parents, that no one is free from the dangers of this insidious problem. No family is automatically protected from the problem—no matter what we do as Christians. Teenagers are always open to experimentation, and this drug is so available and addictive that one exposure can send them in the wrong direction.

What Can We Do?

We need to *evaluate* carefully how we use our freedom in Christ, recognizing that our culture presents some unusual problems that make people particularly vulnerable to addiction of various kinds. We must not overgeneralize, of course. The Scriptures teach that we must not judge those who use their freedom in Christ. We must also realize that there are some cultures where drinking alcoholic beverages, for example, is more acceptable than it is in the United States. In these cultures to abstain completely from alcoholic beverages may offend others and build walls that can hinder our efforts to share Christ.

Even in North America our attitude toward people who drink and smoke can hurt our witness for Christ. I had a conversation with a woman one day who was trying to witness to the people in her office by letting them know she didn't drink. I shared with her that she need not concentrate on letting them know she didn't drink—they knew that simply by her actions. Neither did she have to drink to win them. In our culture people respect people who refuse alcoholic beverages—if it's done properly. She could tactfully refrain and concentrate on building friendships with these non-Christians, looking for opportunities to share with them her personal relationship with Christ, not her non-alcoholic habits.

It's interesting how people are aware of the fact that drinking and Christianity have serious conflicts. While working on this very chapter, I was in Denver, Colorado staying in a motel. At about 5 o'clock that evening I went to the restaurant to get a cup of coffee and to do some work on this material. However, since it was dinner time, they hesitated to seat me in the main dining room and suggested that I go into the bar. "It's dark in there," I said. "I need to be in a place where I can read and study."

They pointed out that I could be seated next to a window. Sure enough, there was a spot where I could see. The sun was still coming in through a large-paned window. So I sat in this little bar with my open Bible, drinking a cup of decaffeinated coffee and researching what the Bible had to say about "not being given to much wine."

Seated behind me were two couples who noticed that I was reading my Bible. I overheard a bit of their conversation, and it was obvious that they were somewhat ill at ease with my presence with a Bible in the bar. Finally one of them asked me what I was doing. To their amazement they found out I was a pastor preparing a message for the weekend. In fact, the door was open for personal witnessing.

I was rather amazed that they did not feel that my Bible and the bar mixed. The very presence of the Word of God made them feel uncomfortable with the environment and their own behavior. In fact, their uncomfortableness eventually caused me some uncomfortableness, and I got up and left.

The point is that those who have worldly views—especially in our culture—know that there are certain things in the Word of God and Christianity that are not compatible with their lifestyle. We don't have to concentrate on telling them—most of them already know! Our task is to share Jesus Christ and not be threatened by their behavior.

We must keep *communication* lines open with our children and youth. This is perhaps our greatest challenge. As I was preparing this material, I was speaking in Salina, Kansas. The very week I was there my son was skiing in Colorado with a group of his friends from Baylor University. In fact, he had put the ski trip together for about thirty college students. While in Salina I discovered I could fly to Denver cheaper than I could fly back to Dallas, so I decided to surprise my son. I flew to Denver, rented a car, and headed for the area of Colorado where they were staying in a condominium. I arrived early in the evening and knew they would already be off the slopes. While looking for them, I stopped at another condominium about two blocks away. I called my son, but didn't let him know where I was. He thought I was in Dallas. We talked for a while, and finally I said, "How about the possibility of skiing with you for a couple of days?" He, of course, was surprised by the question and asked, "What do you mean?"

"Well," I said, "I'm just about two minutes away!" He just about fell off the chair.

Interestingly, the owner of the condominium where I used the telephone made a very interesting comment when she discovered what I was doing. "You're the last person your son is going to want to see!" she said. She was saying that college students on spring break don't want their fathers around.

I was a little surprised by that statement, but it also revealed my naivete. As it turned out, my son welcomed me and actually gave up his bed and insisted that I stay in the condominium that night. "I'm really glad you came, Dad!" he said. "I really want you to meet my friends." We had a delightful two days of skiing together.

I shared this particular experience with someone in our church. "You don't realize how fortunate you are!" she said. "A lot of kids wouldn't want their parents around under those circumstances!"

Frankly, at times I don't really realize how fortunate I am— that my son really likes and respects me. Frankly, I cannot take too much credit for it. Along with many other Christian leaders, I could be in a very different situation—alienated from my children. I simply thank God for His grace and I never want to judge those who have not been as fortunate. I just want to continue to pray that God will protect my children. I only want to help, to comfort others—by sharing sensitively the truths of the Word of God with practical suggestions for following the will of God. For it is in the Word of God that we can find the route to being liked and respected—even by our children.

CHAPTER FOUR

Never Resort to Violence

"He must be . . . not violent." (Titus 1:7)

The very week I was preparing this material, I heard a horror story involving a young man whose parents attend our church. At that time, Scurry lived in Austin, Texas. Unfortunately, at one point in his life, even though a Christian, he had become involved in drugs and alcohol. Fortunately he had since admitted his problem and overcome the habit, and when this event took place, he had been clean for two years. He was attending Alcoholics Anonymous regularly for support and encouragement.

One evening Scurry was attending one of these meetings. He and a friend arrived early. His friend went over and sat on a couch beside a young woman who also attended AA regularly. Behind them was an open window. Hearing some commotion outside, the young woman stood up to see what was happening. At that moment three shots rang out! A man standing outside fired two shots into the back of her head and then turned the gun on himself and blew his own brains out. The man was her former husband.

Scurry's friend was so traumatized by this horrible experience that he immediately threw himself on the floor in the corner of the room and covered his head with a pillow. Another man in the room jumped through the window to pursue the attacker, but found him with the gun, lying on the ground, mortally and violently wounded by his own hand—a victim of his own jealousy and anger. Scurry rushed over to the young woman lying on the floor and tried to administer first aid. His efforts were fruitless. She died thirty minutes later on the way to the hospital.

Subsequently, Scurry called his brother Bruce in Dallas, who in turn related the story to me. "My brother was so upset by this event," Bruce said, "that he couldn't sleep all night. The next evening Scurry turned on the TV to try to forget. He began to watch a relatively mild detective show. But suddenly, the sound of gunshots and sight of people falling wounded became so real and repulsive that he couldn't continue watching." Violence had become real!

A story like this shocks us. It should—but it should not surprise us. When sin entered the world, humanity inherited an incredible capacity toward violence.

The First Murder

Violence in its worst form began with our first parents' eldest son, Cain. He resented his younger brother Abel because God accepted Abel's offering and rejected his own—probably because of Cain's sin and wrongdoing in the first place. God told him, "If you do what is right, will you not be accepted?" (Gen. 4:7)

The Lord then added a very significant warning—one every human being should heed—"But if you do not do what is right, sin is crouching at your door; it desires to have you, but you must master it" (4:7).

Unfortunately, Cain did not heed God's warning. He did not deal with his jealousy and anger. He let the sun go down on his wrath. Whether he planned his brother's death or struck out at him in a moment of rage we're not told, but while they were out in the field alone, "Cain attacked his brother Abel and killed him" (4:8).

Moses' Serious Mistake

Over the years even some of God's choicest servants have allowed their anger to get out of control, leading to violent acts. Moses, for example, killed an Egyptian who was beating one of his Hebrew brothers. Though Moses no doubt felt justified in what he had done—probably because of his high political position in Egypt as well as his heritage as an Israelite—it is clear from the story that he was taking both the law of the land and God's Law into his own hands. Consequently, he brought down on his head the wrath of the King of Egypt and at the same time lost the trust of the very people he was attempting to defend. As a result, he had to flee into the wilderness to escape death himself (Ex. 2:11-15).

David's Horrible Crime

David's crime probably represents the most frightening illustration in Scripture. It demonstrates that even a man after God's heart, a man who could write the beautiful Twenty-third Psalm, can commit violence against another. In a moment of selfish desire, even though he had access to hundreds of other women who in his culture were recognized as his legitimate wives, he used his kingly position and power to take another man's wife into his own bedchamber. Because Bathsheba became pregnant, he tried to cover his sin with an insidious plot. He designed a scheme to have Uriah—Bathsheba's husband—killed on the front lines in battle so that it appeared to be an accidental death.

David paid some horrible consequences for these sins, consequences that plagued him until the day he died. Perhaps the most painful of these consequences was what happened to his own children. His son Amnon raped his own sister Tamar (2 Sam. 13:1-14)—another violent crime that has been around since the Fall. Because of Amnon's sin, David's son Absalom so hated Amnon that after two years of bitterness, he schemed his death (13:22-29). Later Absalom turned against his own father and devised another scheme to turn the Children of Israel against David (15:1-12). And because David himself at times was such a violent man, God actually allowed his son Absalom to turn the hearts of the Children of Israel away from him. Shimei, a member of Saul's family, pronounced a curse on David—a curse David recognized as coming from God (16:5-12).

Though David was intensely repentant for his sin (and God certainly forgave him), he never got away from the consequences of that sin. His family's story is one of the most sordid and sad sagas in all of Scripture. It is filled with horrible violence.

It should not surprise us then that mankind through the centuries has had a propensity toward violence. Violence characterized the first major sin that resulted from our first parents' disobedience in the Garden of Eden, and it has affected some of God's choicest people. The redemptive aspect of David's personality was that he was repentant and truly sorry for his sin. Though he pleaded for mercy, he did not rationalize his wickedness when he totally understood it.

Psalm 51 expresses that repentant heart—which was probably written after he had been confronted by Nathan the Prophet with his sin against Bathsheba and her husband. With a broken heart he wrote:

> Have mercy on me, O God,
>   according to Your unfailing love;
> according to Your great compassion
>   blot out my transgressions.
> Wash away all my iniquity
>   and cleanse me from my sin.

. . . .

Cleanse me with hyssop, and I will be clean;
wash me, and I will be whiter than snow.

. . . .

The sacrifices of God are a broken spirit;
a broken and contrite heart,
O God, You will not despise. (Ps. 51:1-2, 7, 17)

How Does This Apply to Us?

Even though we have been significantly affected by the Laws
of God and the ethics of Christianity, we are increasingly
becoming a violent society. We could talk about the whole
area of sports—hockey, football, and one of the most violent
sports in our society, professional boxing. Have you ever
watched the faces of the people sitting on the front row of a
heavyweight boxing match—particularly when the scene
gets extremely brutal? Both their words and their body
language speak volumes about the emotional satisfaction
they are receiving from the violent scene. In Brazil, men will
not even take women to soccer games because of the violent
speech and behavior in the stadium. How far removed are
we from the Roman Empire's bloody and deadly contests
between men and men or men and beasts?

As I was working on this chapter, I couldn't help but think
about Nazi Germany and the violent acts committed against
six million Jews and many, many others. It became a very
personal time of reflection. I'm German—mostly at least. I
grew up in a German community. Many of my closest friends
were German. Some were even born in Germany and had
moved to the States following the war.

Ethnically, I represent some of the same people who so
casually gunned down millions of Jews or herded them into
gas chambers. I represent people who threw babies against
brick walls and battered their brains out—and then went

home to their own children, held them in their arms, rocked them, and then tucked them into bed.

Are all Germans psychopathic? Mentally sick? Insensitive and cruel? The answer, of course, is no. But we, like all people, are sinners. And we—along with every human being alive—have the same capacity to engage in violence toward our fellow human beings and to follow the leadership of violent men—Hitlers, Mussolinis, and Gaddafis! Maybe these men are sick, but why do men and women who are mentally and emotionally healthy follow them and carry out their orders? The answer is that to a certain degree we are all schizophrenic, in the sense that we have a sin nature that can lead us to do horrible things and overshadow whatever semblance of good that remains in our hearts and personalities because we are made in the image of God.

Chuck Colson makes an interesting point in the July 1983 issue of *Jubilee*.

I discovered a dearth of contemporary writings on sin. After a long search, however, an unlikely source—Mike Wallace of "60 Minutes"—furnished just what I was looking for.

Since Christians are not accustomed to gleaning great theological insights from network TV, I'd better explain.

Introducing a recent story about Nazi Adolf Eichmann, a principal architect of the Holocaust, Wallace posed a central question at the program's outset: "How is it possible . . . for a man to act as Eichmann acted? . . . Was he a monster? A madman? Or was he perhaps something even more terrifying: was he normal?"

Normal? The executioner of millions of Jews normal? Most self-respecting viewers would be outraged at the very thought.

The most startling answer to Wallace's shocking question came in an interview with Yehiel Dinur, a concentration camp survivor who testified against Eichmann at the Nuremburg trials. A film clip from Eichmann's 1961 trial showed Dinur walking into the courtroom, stopping short, seeing Eichmann for the first time since the Nazis had sent him to Auschwitz 18 years earlier. Dinur began to sob uncontrollably, then fainted, collapsing in a heap on the floor as the presiding judicial officer pounded his gavel for order in the crowded courtroom.

Was Dinur overcome by hatred? Fear? Horrid memories?

No; it was none of these. Rather, as Dinur explained to Wallace, all at once he realized Eichmann was not the god-like officer who had sent so many to their deaths. This Eichmann was an ordinary man. "I was afraid about myself," said Dinur. . . . "I saw that I am capable to do this. I am . . . exactly like he."

Wallace's subsequent summation of Dinur's terrible discovery—"Eichmann is in all of us"—is a horrifying statement; but it indeed captures the central truth about man's nature. For as a result of the Fall, sin is in each of us—not just the susceptibility to sin, but sin itself.

The reality of what Chuck Colson pointed out in this editorial came home to me one day in a very personal way. My oldest daughter had a scary experience while driving to work. While pulling up to a stop light, she inadvertently and unintentionally irritated a driver in another car.

The driver my daughter encountered jumped out of his car and ran up to hers and tried to open her door. Fortunately it was locked. He next proceeded to beat his fists against her windows, trying to smash them in. He also pounded the hood and kicked the side of the car—and finally with his bare hands demolished her side-view mirror. As she looked on in horror, she noticed particularly the man's eyes. They were ablaze with fire and hatred—reflecting violent anger. I cringe when I think what he might have done to my daughter had he been able to get inside the car.

But let's get even more specific and practical. Let's talk about what is happening in our society that is affecting our children. Listen to these statistics and observations from the National Coalition on TV Violence, an organization located in Champaign, Illinois. They report:

• Seven out of ten most popular toys on today's market are war toys. The sales of these items are up 600% in the past three years—from $186 million in 1982 to $1.2 billion in 1985.

• NCTV has completed a study of children who play with violent dolls as opposed to nonviolent dolls. Statistics showed a doubling of angry behavior and loss of temper linked to playing with violent dolls.

• Eighty-five percent of all new cartoon programs are war cartoons funded by the various toy companies to promote their line of war toys.

• It is estimated that the average U.S. child will view 250 war cartoon episodes and 800 war-related ads this year on TV. This is the equivalent of 22 days of classroom instruction on prowar behavior.

• The average American is "consuming" 10 to 15 hours of violent entertainment per week in TV viewing.

Another organization, The Family Place, reports the following:

• In Texas, one out of four women experiences domestic violence in her lifetime. Fifteen percent of Texan women are severely and repeatedly abused.

• Nationally, an incident of wife abuse occurs once every 18 seconds.

The Department of Human Resources in Dallas reports the following:

• They receive 250 to 300 calls monthly concerning child abuse.

- Of the above figures, 35 percent represent physical abuse, and 25 percent to 30 percent reflect sexual abuse.
- Eighty to eighty-five percent of abused children are under the age of three.

Similar statistics could be reported in nearly every major city and most states in America.

And finally, one of the most violent tragedies that takes place every day is that an average of 180 babies are "legally" killed every hour in the United States. Legalized abortion is probably one of the greatest crimes against humanity that exists in our society today. In essence how far, then, are we from the crimes of Nazi Germany? How far are we from what was really happening in the Roman Empire? Perhaps in the mind of God, there is very little difference.

As Christians we must be careful to guard our reputations by steering clear of violence. Some Christian parents become violent in their discipline of their children, which is certainly not what God had in mind when He exhorted us to discipline our children. We are not likely to be respected if we fall prey to this kind of behavior.

CHAPTER FIVE

Be Honest in All Relationships

"He must be blameless . . .
not pursuing dishonest gain." (Titus 1:7)

I have an open-line radio program once a week entitled "Let's Talk!" People can visit the "pastor's study" by telephone to talk about any concern they might have. One day a lady called and shared that she and her husband attend a particular church. They had recently been asked by the pastor to serve on a stewardship committee to raise funds for the church. To their amazement they discovered that the church had no budget and published no financial reports. To top it off, they also discovered that the pastor was the only one who knew anything about the church's income and expenditures. Furthermore, he determined and paid his own salary.

In addition to this unfortunate system, in which the pastor was not held accountable financially, the pastor consistently taught prosperity giving—that is, when you give your money to the church, God is obligated to multiply your income. In other words, if you want to get wealthy, be a generous giver!

I'm sure you recognize the problem inherent in this situation. Even if the pastor is an honest man, he is not protecting his reputation nor is he protecting the name of Jesus Christ.

Frankly, I couldn't help but question his integrity, because the moment this couple began to ask about the church's income, how the money was spent, the budget, and how staff salaries were determined, they were given the icy treatment and totally ignored.

Their questions to me by telephone focused on what to do under these circumstances. What was their responsibility to the others in the church? What was their spiritual responsibility to the pastor?

These were tough questions! There are thousands of so-called churches that claim to teach the Word of God and present Jesus Christ as Saviour who follow this same pattern in their approach to finances. In some cases their systems are simply disorganized and sloppy, but their motives are pure and aboveboard. In other cases, there is deliberate secrecy for reasons that are questionable.

To complicate matters, pastors and preachers today have access to the media. Television, for example, multiplies their potential income base tremendously. There are two themes that are constantly presented that open people's pocketbooks faster than any other, prosperity giving and physical healing. In many instances, these themes reflect a misinterpretation of Scripture—a twisting of biblical truth to achieve financial goals. This is a twentieth-century example of what Paul warned against—"pursuing dishonest gain" (Titus 1:7).

A First-Century Problem

There's no question what Paul had in mind when he warned against "pursuing dishonest gain." There were individuals in the New Testament world who were emerging as leaders and taking advantage of Christians financially. Their motives were selfish and sinful. Their tactics were dishonest and manipulative. In fact, Paul explained his concerns about this with a very specific description of these individuals in the latter part of Titus 1. "For there are many rebellious people," he wrote, "mere talkers and deceivers. . . . They must be silenced, because they are ruining whole households by teaching things they ought not to teach—and that for the sake of dishonest gain" (Titus 1:10-11).

Note that this was a problem involving a lot of people. Paul states there were "many"—not just a few dishonest people. Note also that they were not only taking advantage of people, but they were actually teaching *false doctrine* in order to achieve their financial goals.

This problem pervaded the New Testament world. This, of course, was not only a problem in Crete, where Titus was. Everywhere Paul went he encountered dishonesty among false teachers. This is why he included financial integrity as a requirement for spiritual leaders when he wrote to Timothy in Ephesus. He underscored this point for both elders (1 Tim. 3:3) and deacons (3:8). Peter emphasized the same point when he wrote to Christians scattered "throughout Pontus, Galatia, Cappadocia, Asia and Bithynia" (1 Peter 1:1). Speaking to those who were spiritual leaders, he wrote, "Be shepherds of God's flock that is under your care, serving as overseers—not because you must, but because you are willing, as God wants you to be; not greedy for money, but eager to serve; not lording it over those entrusted to you, but being examples to the flock" (5:2-3).

This problem was an extension of an Old Testament problem. What was happening in the New Testament world had also happened in Old Testament days among the people of Israel. This is no doubt one reason why Paul referred to this problem particularly among the "circumcision group" (Titus 1:10). In the midst of horrible apostasy, Jeremiah once wrote, "From the least to the greatest, all are greedy for gain; prophets and priests alike, all practice deceit" (Jer. 6:13). The Lord told the Prophet Ezekiel, "My people come to you, as they usually do, and sit before you to listen to your words, but they do not put them into practice. With their mouths they express devotion, but their hearts are greedy for unjust gain" (Ezek. 33:31). Micah wrote, "They covet fields and seize them, and houses, and take them. They defraud a man of his home, a fellowman of his inheritance" (Micah 2:2). And Habakkuk warned against the same problem—"Woe to him who builds his realm by unjust gain to set his nest on high, to escape the clutches of ruin!" (Hab. 2:9)

Paul then was dealing with a problem that had existed since the dawn of creation—even among God's people. And note also that these kinds of actions are disastrous. The men Paul was writing about to Titus were "ruining whole households" (Titus 1:11), not only because of their false teaching, but also because many of these people would either follow their evil ways and become like them or become so disillusioned with Christianity that they would revert to their pagan ways.

Paul had little patience with these false and dishonest teachers. "They must be silenced," he wrote (Titus 1:11). "Rebuke them sharply, so that they will be sound in the faith" (1:13).

This problem is often condemned in Scripture. Financial integrity is a mark of a mature disciple of Jesus Christ. Accordingly, dishonest gain is often condemned in Scripture. Listen to these biblical warnings and commands:

● "A greedy man brings trouble to his family, but he who hates bribes will live" (Prov. 15:27).

● "Whoever loves money never has money enough; whoever loves wealth is never satisfied with his income. This too is meaningless" (Ecc. 5:10).

● "Like a partridge that hatches eggs it did not lay is the man who gains riches by unjust means. When his life is half gone, they will desert him, and in the end he will prove to be a fool" (Jer. 17:11).

● "For the love of money is a root of all kinds of evil. Some people, eager for money, have wandered from the faith and pierced themselves with many griefs" (1 Tim. 6:10).

● "Your gold and silver are corroded. Their corrosion will testify against you and eat your flesh like fire. You have hoarded wealth in the last days" (James 5:3).

A New Testament Principle

Having stated the New Testament problem, let's look at a very important New Testament principle—one that is easily abused by both Christian leaders as well as the rest of the body of Christ.

The principle stated: Spiritual leaders are to be remunerated for their efforts, and God's people are to provide this financial support.

This principle has its basis in the Old Testament pattern of tithing. The Levites were the people who served the rest of the people in spiritual matters; they were in charge of the tabernacle. The members of the tribe of Levi were to be provided for by the other eleven tribes, who were to give a tenth of all they produced, both flocks and crops, to meet this special need (Lev. 27:30-33; Num. 18:21).

In turn, a tenth of what the Levites received was to be given to the priests—those who ministered in a special way *in* the tabernacle. Thus all of those in Israel who cared for the spiritual needs of God's people were cared for by the rest of Israel. To violate this Law of God in Old Testament days led to serious consequences. God spoke to the children of Israel through Malachi, saying,

"Will a man rob God? Yet you rob Me. But you ask, 'How do we rob You?' In tithes and offerings. You are under a curse—the whole nation of you—because you are robbing Me. Bring the whole tithe into the storehouse, that there may be food in My house. Test Me in this," says the

Lord Almighty, "and see if I will not throw open the floodgates of heaven and pour out so much blessing that you will not have room enough for it. I will prevent pests from devouring your crops, and the vines in your fields will not cast their fruit," says the Lord Almighty. "Then all the nations will call you blessed, for yours will be a delightful land," says the Lord Almighty. (Mal. 3:8-12)

Our New Testament principle emerges from this Old Testament pattern. When Paul wrote to the Corinthians, he raised a series of questions:

Who serves as a soldier at his own expense? Who plants a vineyard and does not eat of its grapes? Who tends a flock and does not drink of the milk? Do I say this merely from a human point of view? Doesn't the Law say the same thing? (1 Cor. 9:7-8)

Paul then answers these questions:

For it is written in the Law of Moses: "Do not muzzle an ox while it is treading out the grain." Is it about oxen that God is concerned? Surely He says this for us, doesn't He? Yes, this was written for us, because when the plowman plows and the thresher threshes, they ought to do so in the hope of sharing in the harvest. (1 Cor. 9:9-10)

Paul then makes the specific application to those who minister the Gospel and the Word of God.

If we have sown spiritual seed among you, is it too much if we reap a material harvest from you? If others have this right of support from you, shouldn't we have it all the more? (1 Cor. 9:11-12)

Writing to the Galatians, Paul made this point very practical. "Anyone who receives instruction in the word must share all good things with his instructor" (Gal. 6:6). Paul also wrote to Timothy,

> The elders who direct the affairs of the church well are worthy of double honor, especially those whose work is preaching and teaching. For the Scripture says, "Do not muzzle the ox while it is treading out the grain," and "The worker deserves his wages." (1 Tim. 5:17-18)

There's no question what Paul had in mind here. The Greek word translated "double honor" means literally "honorarium" or "money." To make sure they didn't misunderstand his point, Paul refers to "wages." Paul is teaching that spiritual leaders who minister in the church and serve other people—particularly in teaching them the Word of God—are to be cared for by the people to whom they minister. In fact, to be fed the Word of God and not respond by meeting the needs of those who are ministering to you is a violation of the will of God.

The problem in the first-century world was that so-called spiritual leaders were abusing this New Testament principle. They even twisted God's Word and taught false doctrine to make money. This is why Paul insisted that spiritual leaders in the church not be guilty of "pursuing dishonest gain." Financial integrity is to be a mark of maturity for *all* followers of Jesus Christ, no matter what our vocational calling. Without it, we will be neither liked or respected by Christians or non-Christians. Integrity is central to building a good reputation God's way.

Twentieth-Century Problems

Unfortunately, the first-century problem Paul was speaking to in his letter to Titus has not gone away. It has persisted and pervaded every culture of the world since the time of Christ. It exists today in all of its ugliness, particularly in the American culture, whose roots have strong ties to the values and teachings of Christianity.

Pursuing dishonest gain today. At the beginning of this chapter I illustrated the way this problem has emerged in the American culture among Christian leaders. Prosperity giving and healing are taught in order to motivate people to give.

Don't misunderstand! I believe God does bless us when we are faithful stewards financially, and I believe God does heal. But what is often taught by many television and radio evangelists and local church pastors is a perversion of these great biblical truths. It is no wonder the world watches these antics and concludes that most Christian programs are money-raising schemes—means of "dishonest gain."

The sad part is that it makes it extremely difficult for the many—and there are thousands—Christian leaders who want to be totally honest and true to the Word of God. In fact, it makes it very difficult even to talk about money, a subject the Bible speaks to again and again.

I was talking with a friend of mine the very week I was preparing this chapter. She has a quality Christian radio program that was being aired on a large radio station on the West Coast. However, it followed a program featuring a well-known radio and television preacher in the United States. She heard this man (this time on television) offer a set of cassette tapes valued at about $20. He was selling them for $100. Speaking forcefully to the audience, as the toll-free number appeared on the screen, he told them that God had told him to tell them that they were supposed to buy this set of tapes. My friend was so disturbed with this man's methodology that she pulled her own radio program off the radio station he was also heard on. She did not want even to be associated with either this man's theology or his methodology. I admire my friend's integrity.

As a pastor I have personally given a lot of thought to this matter. Our elders have insisted on careful financial records and financial accountability in our church. I personally give a detailed financial report every month to our board of elders, accounting for every penny spent. There are no secrets. To me this is a must to protect my own reputation, the reputation of this church, and the reputation of the Lord Jesus Christ.

There is another factor I'll share openly. When we launched the Center for Church Renewal ministry (an organization I direct to help launch and renew churches, families, and marriages), I recommended a procedure to the board whereby all income that I generated through speaking in addition to my regular salary would go into a special ministry and travel fund in the Center for Church Renewal account. In other words, I wanted a system whereby I did not personally keep money that I had generated through speaking—even though I often do it on my own time.

The reasons for this proposal (which the board accepted) are very simple. I don't want to be guilty of a conflict of interest. I don't even want to be tempted in that area. And I certainly don't want people ever to question my integrity in that area—for if they do it will be a bad reflection on the church, the ministry of the Center for Church Renewal, and our Lord Jesus Christ Himself. Frankly, I'd much rather give up certain rights that may hurt the cause of Christ than be a stumbling block to others. This was Paul's model for Christian leaders throughout the centuries. He often gave up his own financial rights in order to be free from any criticism (1 Cor. 9). It is clear from Scripture that we are to imitate his life as he imitated the life of Jesus Christ (1 Cor. 11:1).

Financial integrity is, of course, a characteristic of all mature Christians, no matter what their vocations. There is no place for dishonesty in any aspect of a Christian's life. In a world where lying and cheating have often become the norm in the business world, every Christian must take a stand for what is right. We must not compromise integrity. It is a basic quality of life which we must develop if we want people to like and respect us. Even if they don't like us, they will usually respect us.

The other side of the coin. There is another side of this picture that affects every member of the body of Christ. The Scriptures—as we've seen—clearly teach that we are to minister in material ways to people who minister to us in spiritual ways. There are, however, many Christians who sit in churches week after week but who do not participate in a regular and systematic program of giving to care for the needs of those who minister to them and their families. Consequently, there is often a shortage of church funds to carry on God's work. The saddest part is that there are thousands of Christian leaders who are woefully underpaid, simply because Christian people are not fulfilling their God-ordained responsibility, the principle God established from the beginning.

This ought not to be. Many people do this because they have not been taught good stewardship; they are not aware of their biblical responsibility. However, there are many people who are aware of this responsibility but who continue in selfishness. This is just as wrong as dishonest gain. We are "robbing God," to quote Malachi. If the Children of Israel were robbing God under law, how much more so are we robbing God under grace? The Bible clearly teaches that we should regularly and joyously set apart a part of our income in keeping with the way in which God has blessed us (1 Cor. 16:1-2; 2 Cor. 8–9). For many of us in our culture, this will take us far beyond the ten percent that was required in Israel. Ten percent should only be a starting point for many American Christians. We must not take advantage of the grace of God. True, we're not under law, but grace should teach us to respond with hearts of love and gratitude.

Some Personal Questions

We need to ask ourselves how we're measuring up in the area of financial integrity. Ask yourself from time to time:

● Am I maintaining financial integrity in all my relationships, both with Christians and non-Christians?

● Am I keeping myself from being manipulated and deceived by religious hucksters? (The only way to do this is to invest your money in people and organizations you have come to know and trust through close association and trustworthy recommendations. Do not give to organizations that are not open and straightforward regarding their financial resources and policies.)

● Am I faithfully supporting those who minister to me in spiritual things?

● Am I a good steward of all that God has given me—my time, talents, and gifts?

If you can answer these questions positively, you are on your way to building a good reputation.

CHAPTER SIX

Use What You Have to Serve Others

"He must be hospitable." (Titus 1:8)

Several years ago I was conducting a seminar based on the characteristics for maturity outlined in 1 Timothy 3 and Titus 1. Two men were attending who were in upper management in one of the large steel mills in Gary, Indiana. Both of these men were brand new Christians. I could tell from their body language and verbal responses that these two men were really tracking with me as I shared this biblical material.

During one of the coffee breaks, I discovered why they were so intrigued and interested. "I've heard of Timothy," one of them said, "but this Titus guy—I've never heard of him at all!" The other man agreed. I knew immediately I was interacting not only with new Christians but with two men who knew very little about the Bible. However, they were extremely experienced as leaders in a large secular organization. What I was sharing was brand new—from a biblical point of view. They had never read these passages. In fact, they didn't know these characteristics were in the Bible.

I then discovered *why* they were so interested in the content of the seminar. As upper-management people they were responsible for hiring middle-management personnel to occupy positions in their company.

"This is fascinating!" one man responded. "I've never studied these biblical reflections of maturity, but through practical experience we've learned that these qualities are exactly what we're looking for in our middle-management team. We don't want a man with a bad reputation—a man who is cheating on his wife, a man whose children don't respect and honor him. We don't want a man who is overbearing and self-centered, or a person who is always losing his cool and hurting other employees' feelings, and we certainly don't want a man who is addicted to chemicals of any kind, or who is given to violence. Naturally we don't want a man who is dishonest and would take advantage of the company financially." These men went on to point out that Paul's maturity profile was essentially the same as what they had been using in their own selection process for hiring leaders in that company.

I was as intrigued with their comments as they were with mine. Here were very experienced professional men who had just recently become Christians. Knowing nothing about the Bible, they had learned from experience that there are certain characteristics that would make a bad leader—in the home and in the factory. On the other hand, there are certain qualities that make a good leader. In essence, they were saying that these characteristics or their lack reflect a mature or immature personality—no matter what the position in life, whether Christian or non-Christian.

"Amazing!" I thought. But upon reflection, it really isn't that amazing. God authored the Bible through men like Paul. It is logical that there is a common base for recognizing maturity in all human beings. Being the source of all truth, God outlined for us a maturity profile—a profile that will hopefully enable us to win respect and love.

Since then I've noticed that there are some people who

are not true Christians (that is, they have not put their faith in Christ for personal salvation) who are yet in some respects more respected than true Christians. That is unfortunate and tragic! Of all people, Christians ought to have good reputations. Those of us who don't are certainly not bearing a good witness for our Lord and Saviour Jesus Christ. Furthermore, that seminar experience taught me that non-Christians recognize whether or not we are mature, even though they don't understand fully what the Bible says about maturity and even though they don't understand the divine resources we have as believers to develop that maturity. This also taught me why it is so important for Christians to demonstrate with their lives what they profess with their lips.

This brings us once again to what Paul wrote to Titus. Let's review:

What causes a bad reputation? (Titus 1:7)
● Being overbearing
● Being quick-tempered
● Being given to much wine
● Being violent
● Pursuing dishonest gain

What causes a good reputation? According to Titus 1:8, being hospitable will help establish a good reputation. Besides Paul's reference to being hospitable in his letter to Timothy (1 Tim. 3:2)—which includes basically the same qualities as his letter to Titus—there are three other important letters in the New Testament that include the same positive personality trait. Perhaps more than any other, we can practice this quality, being hospitable, to win respect and develop a good reputation. People are attracted to Christians who reach out to others in this way. They will both respect and like us as we practice hospitality.

"Practice Hospitality"—Romans 12:13

The context of this exhortation makes it clear what Paul is talking about. These Christians were to "share with God's people who are in need" (Rom. 12:13). The very word *hospitable* means being generous and caring toward others. That's why we call our medical centers "hospitals"; they are places where we can help people who are physically and emotionally hurting.

The church too is to be a "hospital"—a place where Christian share with one another what they have to meet each other's needs. This may involve providing funds for people who have emergency financial needs. In our own church we have a "love fund" for this purpose—a fund we try to monitor carefully to make sure that it is used to show hospitality. This may also mean giving to meet the special needs of those who minister to us in the Word of God. That's why when Paul wrote to the Galatians, he stated specifically, "Anyone who receives instructions in the word must share all good things with his instructor" (Gal. 6:6). It may also involve using our homes and resources to minister to others—just to share love and friendship. It certainly involves reaching out to help others outside our own local churches.

Several other places in the New Testament help clarify what Paul had in mind. In fact, the context in his letter to Titus is significant. A Christian is not to pursue "dishonest gain," but rather to "be hospitable." This contrast is not by accident. What Paul wrote was certainly orchestrated by the Holy Spirit.

Paul emphasized the same point in his letter to the Ephesians, but he became even more specific. "He who has been stealing [that is, pursuing dishonest gain] must steal no longer, but must work, doing something useful with his own hands, that he may have something to share with those in need [show hospitality]" (Eph. 4:28).

I was particularly thrilled the very week I was writing this chapter. I received word regarding what nine men who attend Fellowship Bible Church of San Antonio were planning to do. This church had been started a little over a year before, under the auspices of our own church renewal organization. A Dallas businessman initially helped fund this church-planting project. A group of men were planning to fly to a remote jungle camp in Ecuador to share of themselves and their resources to construct a facility for a very special missionary.

Let me share the background. In 1956 a shock wave was sent around the world as five missionaries lay on the banks of the Curaray River in Ecuador, murdered by savage Auca Indians. Two years later, Rachael Saint, a sister of one of the martyred men, along with Dayuma, a runaway Auca Indian girl, courageously walked back into the tribe under God's guidance and protection. The result has been no less than earth-shattering.

The first rough draft of the Auca New Testament was scheduled to be completed by 1988. Rachael has spent most of the last twenty-eight years living among the tribe. In conjunction with Wycliffe Bible Translators, she has learned the language, reduced it to writing, taught the people how to read, and was working to place the completed New Testament in their hands—which they call "God's carving." This Saint among savages has seen all of her brother's killers converted to Jesus Christ and three of those men pastor Auca churches.

During the time Rachael has lived among this tribe, she has had no running water, no bathroom facilities, no stove or conveniences we call necessities. At the age of seventy-two, two hours of her day has been spent just boiling water, plus untold precious time just making do. This valuable time could be spent completing her translation work.

This crew of men from Fellowship Bible Church of San Antonio planned to fly to this remote jungle camp to spend

10 days constructing facilities to lighten Rachael's load so the job of translation could be finished on time.

The materials for the project were flown into the jungle by Missionary Aviation Fellowship and constructed on the site by these nine men, who personally raised the money to complete the project.

That, my friends, is carrying out Paul's exhortation in Romans 12:13, "Share with God's people who are in need. Practice hospitality."

"Offer Hospitality to One Another"—1 Peter 4:9

Peter too exhorts Christians to practice hospitality, but he adds another important dimension. He wrote, "Offer hospitality to one another without grumbling."

Christians are to practice hospitality with the right spirit. That's why Paul wrote to the Corinthians, "Each man should give what he has decided in his heart to give, not reluctantly or under compulsion, for God loves a cheerful giver" (2 Cor. 9:7).

I remember reading a beautiful story that illustrates this kind of hospitality. Sam Foss was an enthusiastic traveler as well as a writer, and on one of his trips through rustic England, he came to a small unpainted house that stood on top of a fairly steep hill. He was weary and thirsty. He noticed that at the side of the road was crude signpost finger pointing to a well-worn path and a sign that read, "Come in and have a cool drink." Following the path a short distance, he found a spring of ice-cold water, above which hung an old-fashioned gourd dipper. On a bench nearby was a basket of summer apples with another sign: "Help yourself."

Foss' curiosity was aroused. He sought out the old couple who lived in the little house and questioned them about the signs and the fruit. He learned that they were childless and that their poor farm yielded them a scant living. But because they had such and abundance of cold spring water and fruit, they felt rich and wanted to share it with anyone who might pass that way. "We're too poor to give money to charity," the old gentleman said. "But we thought maybe in this way we could add our mite and do something for folks who pass our way." This experience was the basis for Foss' beautiful poem, "The House by the Side of the Road."

"Do Not Forget to Entertain Strangers"—Hebrews 13:2

The words *entertain strangers* literally refer to "showing hospitality." Again the context is enlightening—"Keep on loving each other as brothers. Do not forget to entertain strangers for by so doing some people have entertained angels without knowing it. Remember those in prison as if you were their fellow prisoners, and those who are mistreated as if you yourselves were suffering" (Heb. 13:1-3).

We all need a word of caution here. There are people who purposely take advantage of Christians, particularly because they know that they are, generally speaking, caring and generous. Over the years I've experienced this personally, and I must admit I've made some bad decisions. In short, I've been taken! But I've learned over the years to control my emotions—at least to a certain extent—and ferret out what is a real, honest need.

Not too long ago I was sitting in my favorite doughnut shop. Next to me was a girl my wife and I had tried to befriend and had gotten to know quite well. Her life has been a disaster. She's a divorcee with several children. Since her divorce, it was obvious she'd been "living around" with guys she had met. She wasn't very secretive about her private life. To add to her plight, though she is certainly intelligent, she is very uneducated. In fact, she has never learned to read.

As I came into the doughnut shop that morning, I sat down beside her and began to plan my day. At first we exchanged hellos as we normally do, and then I went about my business.

Several minutes later she leaned over and quietly asked me

if I could lend her twenty dollars to fill up her car with gas. "I'll pay it back," she said, "as soon as I get my next paycheck."

My heart was immediately moved. I went for my billfold, but then realized I only had enough money with me to pay for a doughnut and a cup of coffee. "I'm sorry," I said. "I don't have any money except enough to pay my bill, but if I did I'd help you out!" I probably would have, and I probably would never have gotten the money back. That, of course, would not have been a disaster, but had I given her the money, it probably wouldn't have been the wisest thing to do. It would have only reinforced her irresponsibility.

Later, when I was a little more objective, I thought about several things. First, she had enough money—and always has—for cigarettes. She's a chain-smoker and had plenty of cigarettes that morning. Second, she commented later in our conversation that she should have been at work, but was running late—but she didn't seem to care much. She continued to sit at the counter, smoke up a storm, eat doughnuts, and drink coffee. And third, I thought, *I know I'm supposed to show hospitality because I might be entertaining an angel unawares, but this girl ain't no angel!*

There are ways to determine true needs and to discover if people are trustworthy. The writer of Hebrews is not teaching us that we should be indiscreet and respond to everybody who asks for a handout. There are people who are irresponsible and downright manipulative. It would not be the loving thing to do to allow them to continue with this kind of behavior. We should be cautious.

But the Bible is teaching that we should care about those in need, even if they are people we don't know. Let us not exclude those who have real needs! By sharing even a cup of cold water, we are sharing in effect with Jesus Christ Himself (Mark 9:41). Christians are to be generous and hospitable. This is one of the outstanding marks of Christian maturity. I believe that is why Paul lists this first as one of the positive qualities that reflects Christian maturity and develops a good reputation.

If you want people to like and respect you, show hospitality. Furthermore, it's a wonderful example to other Christians who need to do the same thing.

CHAPTER SEVEN

Love What Is Good

"He must be one who loves what is good." (Titus 1:8)

There is an intriguing Jewish legend regarding the creation story. It seems that when God was about to create man, He took into His counsel the angels who stood about the throne. "Don't create him," said the angel of justice, "for if You do, he will commit all kinds of wickedness against his fellowman; he will be hard and cruel and dishonest and unrighteous."

"Don't create him," said the angel of truth, "for he will be false and deceitful to his fellowman—and even to You."

The angel of holiness spoke next. "Don't create him," he warned, "for man will follow that which is impure in Your sight and dishonor You to Your face."

Then the angel of mercy stepped forward and said, "Create him, our Heavenly Father, for when he sins and turns from the path of right and truth and holiness, I will take him tenderly by the hand, and speak loving words to him, and then lead him back to You" (Paul Lee Tan, *Encyclopedia of 7,700 Illustrations,* BMH Books, p. 493).

Though this story is a legend, it does reflect what has happened since God created the human race. That's understandable, because the legend was written from the perspective of history. Men and women have created all kinds of wickedness against their fellow human beings. They *have* become hard and cruel and dishonest and unrighteous. They *have* become deceitful to both man and God, and no one can argue against the fact that impurity and immorality have existed throughout history.

But history also reveals that there was an "angel of mercy." God did send His Son to redeem us from our sins and to make it possible for us to turn from following after unrighteousness to do that which is right and truthful and holy. This is why Paul says that a mark of a mature disciple is "one who loves what is good" (Titus 1:8).

An Overview

philagathos	A lover of what is good
philoxenos	A lover of hospitality
philautos	A lover of oneself
philarguros	A lover of money
philedonos	A lover of pleasure
aphilagathos	Not a lover of what is good

This quality of life described with six words in English is expressed by one basic and very descriptive word in the language of the New Testament. It's the word *philagathos*. The first part of this word comes from the word *phileo*, which is the Greek word meaning "to love" or "to desire someone or something." It involves emotion and affection.

When Paul described a mature Christian as one who "loves what is good," he was referring to an individual who is a lover of good people and things. He or she desires to have fellowship with people who are good and wants to focus his or her desire on things that are good.

There are some very interesting relationships between this

word and some of the other words Paul used to describe maturity and immaturity. First of all, in Titus 1:8 this word, *philagathos,* immediately follows the word *philoxenos,* which literally means "a lover of hospitality," or more specifically, "a lover of guests or strangers." This is the quality of maturity we looked at in the last chapter. So by penning just two Greek words, Paul covered a lot of territory in describing a mature follower of Jesus Christ.

We can look much more specifically at what Paul meant by "being one who loves what is good" by looking at a paragraph he wrote in his second letter to Timothy—2 Timothy 3:1-5. In this passage Paul described the positive quality of loving what is good by describing a person living an opposite kind of lifestyle. "But mark this," Paul warned. "There will be terrible times in the last days. People will be lovers of themselves"—not *philagathos* (a lover of good) but *philautos* (a lover of oneself). These people will not be lovers of hospitality nor lovers of good things. They love themselves.

Paul goes on: they are "lovers of money"—not *philoxenos* (lovers of hospitality) and not *philagathos* (lovers of good things), but *philarguros*—lovers of money (vs. 2). Third, they are "lovers of pleasure"—*philedonos* (vs. 4). Paul writes in the latter part of verse 3 that these people are *aphilagathos*, "not lovers of the good," rather than *philagathos.*

So Paul very crisply and with three very descriptive words in Greek describes a person who does *not* love what is good:

- *philautos*—"A lover of oneself"
- *philarguros*—"A lover of money"
- *philedonos*—"A lover of pleasure"

Anyone who is devoted to these things is not a "lover of good people and good things"—the quality Paul lists in his letter to Titus.

With this overall perspective, let's look even more specifically at these negative characteristics, which will bring into relief what Paul meant by being a Christian who "loves what is good."

A Closer Look

As we look at each of these negative characteristics and try to understand them, it is very important that we separate what is good from what is bad. To do this, it helps to look at what Paul *doesn't* mean in order to understand what he *does* mean.

"Lovers of themselves." That we shouldn't be lovers of ourselves does *not* mean that we shouldn't think well of ourselves. We need self-respect; we cannot function as mature persons without it. It's basic to having a good self-image. In fact, without it we will not be able to love others as we should.

This is a very important observation, because some Christians feel guilty when they feel good about themselves. Let it be said for all to hear—Christians who are living in the will of God should, of all people in the world, feel good about themselves. We're God's children; we are heirs together with Christ. We have been redeemed and forgiven of our sins. We were created in God's image to begin with, and though that image was marred by sin, it can be restored; we have the resources to become more and more conformed to the image of Jesus Christ.

What then *does* Paul mean? A Christian who loves himself in the way Paul is talking about focuses on himself rather than on others. He is a victim of the "I," "me," and "mine" syndrome. He is self-involved and self-oriented. His needs are central in all that he does. He is driven by self-interest. In short, he's selfish.

Someone has penned the following words:

Sometimes when you're feeling important,
Sometimes when your ego's in bloom,

Sometime when you take it for granted
You're the best qualified in the room;
Sometimes when you feel that your going
Would leave an unfillable hole,
Just follow these simple instructions
And see how they humble your soul.
Take a bucket and fill it with water
Put your hand in it up to the wrist,
Pull it out, and the hole that's remaining
Is the measure of how you'll be missed.
You can splash all you want when you enter,
You may stir up the water galore;
But stop, and you'll find that in no time
It looks quite the same as before.
The moral in this quaint example
Is to do just the best that you can;
Be proud of yourself, but remember
There's no indispensable man. (Tan, *Illustrations,* pp. 261-262, 771)

Though I may not agree in every respect with the "theology" in this poem, I will have to agree with the principle involved—though I am very important to God and to the Body of Christ, I must not think more highly of myself than I ought to think (Rom. 12:3). Someone else has said, "The smallest package we have ever seen is a man wrapped up in himself."

"Lovers of money." Anyone who has a correct perspective on what the Bible teaches knows that Paul is not condemning having money. Neither did he condemn people who have money. Rather he is warning people who *love* money, for "the love of money is the root of all kinds of evil" (1 Tim. 6:10), not having money in itself.

The problem is that it is easy to love money. Jesus warned against it, stating that it is often very difficult (not impossible) for rich people to enter the kingdom of God. The reason is that they find it very hard to shift their affection away from their material possessions and to acknowledge that they need God.

Paul also minced no words in warning against the tendencies that come when people accumulate material possessions. Writing to Timothy, he said in no uncertain terms, "People who want to get rich fall into temptation and a trap and into many foolish and harmful desires that plunge men into ruin and destruction" (1 Tim. 6:9).

The late Robert Horton made an insightful observation. He said that "the greatest lesson he learned from life was that people who set their minds and hearts on money are equally disappointed whether they get it or whether they don't" (Tan, *Illustrations,* p. 830).

"Lovers of pleasure." This negative characteristic is, of course, interrelated with the two we just looked at. First, it is impossible to experience pleasure apart from ourselves— and self-love *does* give pleasure. That's why people become "lovers of themselves." Second, people become "lovers of money" because money also provides some kind of pleasure. It becomes a *means* to pleasure.

Again, we must understand the positive aspects of this concept. God Himself created the capacity for pleasure. Life would be miserable without it. Do you think Adam experienced any pleasure the first time he saw Eve? You bet he did! Do you think Adam and Eve enjoyed all the delectable fruits and vegetables that God created in the Garden of Eden? Absolutely! God created those things for His people to enjoy. Do you think Adam and Eve experienced any pleasure when they looked at all the beautiful things that God had created— the trees, the beautiful bushes, the variety of animals that graced the landscape? Of course they did. God created all things for us to richly enjoy.

When Israel was ready to enter the Promised Land, God

spoke through Moses, saying, "Hear, O Israel, and be careful to obey so that it will go well with you and that you may increase greatly in a land flowing with milk and honey, just as the Lord, the God of your fathers, promised you" (Deut. 6:3). The place God had created for Israel was to be a place of security, enjoyment, and pleasure.

But something happened to pleasure. It began when sin entered the world. We have once again taken what God has created to be good and for His glory and turned it into something that is wrong and evil. What was designed for marriage, we use illegitimately. What was designed for sustenance, we use to gorge ourselves. Pleasure can become an end in itself, and it can be used in purely selfish, sinful ways that violate the will of God. Pleasure by itself is a dead-end street!

The Key to Balance

In the passage we've looked at in 2 Timothy, Paul gives us the key to balance, the key that unlocks the door to God's will in these matters. In the last days, Paul wrote, people will be "lovers of themselves," "lovers of money," and "lovers of pleasure," rather than "lovers of God" (*philotheos*). Here Paul uses another Greek word, rich in meaning and comprehensive in application. It is our love for God that can put everything in proper perspective. This is why Jesus said that all the commandments could be summarized with this statement, " 'Love the Lord your God with all your heart and with all your soul and with all your mind.' This is the first and greatest commandment. And the second is like it: 'Love your neighbor as yourself.' All the Law and the Prophets hang on these two commandments" (Matt. 22:37-40).

You see, if I love God as I should, I will live within His will as He has revealed it in the Word of God. Jesus reinforced this concept when He said to the disciples, "As the Father has loved Me, so have I loved you. Now remain in My love. If you obey My commands, you will remain in My love, just as I have obeyed My Father's commands and remain in His love. I have told you this so that My joy may be in you and that your joy may be complete" (John 15:9-11). The only way to true happiness and lasting joy is to live within the will of God. Then and only then, all that God has created for us to enjoy will really become fulfilling.

How Should These Truths Affect My Life?

In Paul's second letter to Timothy, he is describing a pagan mentality. People had turned totally away from God. They did not love what is good. In fact, they were openly hostile to Christianity and its values.

Sound familiar? This passage describes to a great extent what has happened in our own society. Today we live in a society that is rapidly becoming post-Christian. People have become "lovers of themselves," "lovers of money," and "lovers of pleasure" rather than "lovers of God." This is a reality—and as Christians we must face that reality.

The question every Christian has to face, however, is, To what extent am I allowing my life to conform to the world's attitudes and actions? To what extent do I focus on myself, my material possessions, and the pleasures of this life? How can I know?

The extent to which I love God and reflect that love by doing His will revealed in the Word of God is also the degree to which I love what is good. Therefore, the real question is, Do I really love God? If you want people to like and respect you, then love what is good.

A Final Word

In the process of his own spiritual journey, Chuck Colson wrote a book entitled *Loving God* (Zondervan). It resulted from what he called a "period of spiritual dryness" in his own life. During that time he was captured by a series of lectures by R.C. Sproul on the holiness of God. He was further prompted to read more on the subject and to interview Christians regarding how they felt about their love for God. The results of this process motivated him to write *Loving God.* His burden is expressed in the introduction to the book, and it is a fitting conclusion to this chapter.

Seeing the desperate hunger in the culture, and realizing how much we as the people of God need to love God, the message of this book was urgently pressed upon me. To use a rather strange, but perhaps appropriate, analogy, I saw a need to attempt to do for the Gospel what Lenin did for Marx.

Though frequently thought of as an arm-waving, fiery revolutionary, Karl Marx was for most of his life a thinker, a theoretician. There was no great workers' revolution during his lifetime, and after his death in 1883, Marxism seemed destined to take its place as just another philosophy spawned by the fertile minds of the nineteenth century. Indeed, it probably would have, were it not for Lenin, a young Russian who voraciously devoured the ideas of Engels and Marx and became a Marxist in 1889.

Three years later, Lenin published *What Is To Be Done?* in which he spelled out the absolute of action, of taking Marx's theories and applying them to life. That book and Lenin's tireless labor inspired a handful of professional revolutionaries who within a few years turned Russia upside down. Lenin's passionate singlemindedness, his absolute commitment and application of Marx's principles changed not only his own country, but today, less than a hundred years later, has enslaved over half the world.

My question then, for individual believers and thus the church, is this: do we view our faith as a magnificent philosophy or a living truth; as an abstract, sometimes academic theory or a living Person for whom we are prepared to lay down our lives? The most destructive and tyrannical movements of the twentieth century, Communism and Nazism, have resulted from fanatics singlemindedly applying fallible philosophies. What would happen if we were actually to apply God's truth for the glory of His kingdom?

The result would be a world turned upside down, revolutionized by the power of God working through individual Christians and the church as a whole.

But we will only be weak and stumbling believers and a crippled church unless and until we truly apply God's Word—that is, until we truly love Him and act on that love. (pp. 16–17)

CHAPTER EIGHT

Maintain Self-control

"He must be . . . one . . . who is self-controlled." (Titus 1:8)

During a speech to the senior class, a college president made this astute observation. "It gets easier," he said, "for men and women to control the universe. But, it seems to get harder and harder for human beings to control themselves."

One of the most attractive characteristics of a mature Christian is self-control—*sophron* in the Greek. This is a very interesting word in the New Testament. It comes from the verb *sophroneo,* which means "to be self-controlled." More specifically it means "to be of a sound mind." Various English words are used to communicate what scriptural writers had in mind—to be "discreet," "sensible," "sober," and "temperate." In the *New International Version* in Titus 1:8 it's translated "self-controlled."

Let's look at one of several instances where Paul uses a form of the word *sophron,* the one that probably describes best what Paul had in mind when he talked about being self-controlled.

Paul instructed Titus to share certain things with various groups of people—those seeking leadership positions in the church, older men, older women, younger women, and young men in the church. It's this last group we want to look at particularly, although self-control is important for all of these groups. But when he instructed Titus regarding his ministry to young men, he gave a more detailed description of what is involved (Titus 2:6-8).

"Encourage the young men," Paul wrote, "to be self-controlled" (vs. 6). He then elaborated on what he meant. "In everything set them an example by doing what is good. In your teaching show integrity, seriousness and soundness of speech that cannot be condemned, so that those who oppose you may be ashamed because they have nothing bad to say about us" (2:7-8).

Modeling Self-control

There are some biblical truths that can be taught didactically, such as who Jesus is, what God is like, how to be saved, and many other Bible doctrines. But there are some things that must be taught by both instruction and example. In fact, without example some words are meaningless. *Self-control* is one of those words. Thus Paul tells Titus that *he* must demonstrate self-control if young men are to learn to demonstrate that same quality in their lives.

I had a very personal and meaningful experience a couple of weeks before I was writing this chapter. I was having breakfast with my son Kenton, at that time a sophomore at Baylor University. Our conversation with each other that morning reached a deeper level than ever before. We were talking about a series of letters that I had written him—a series that I began when he was in high school and involved with Teen Missions overseas. I eventually finished the series during his freshman year in college while he was counseling at a sports-oriented Christian camp. The letters were based on Paul's words to Timothy—"Don't let anyone look down on you because you are young, but set an example for the

believers in speech, in life, in love, in faith and in purity"
(1 Tim. 4:12). There were seven letters in all, and each was
based upon one of the qualities outlined in this verse.

At one point in our conversation, Kenton shared with me
something he had never shared before. "Dad," he said, "I
want you to know you're my model, and I want to be like
you." I knew he wasn't saying that he necessarily wanted to
be a pastor or even have some kind of full-time Christian
ministry. He was talking about something far more significant—something more important than our vocations. As he
went on to explain what he meant, I knew that he was talking
about what we are as people.

I had two reactions to that statement. One was immediate;
the other has continued to occupy my mind and heart. My
immediate reaction was deep gratitude—particularly when
he explained what he saw in my life that he felt reflected
Jesus Christ. In fact, I was rather overwhelmed with gratitude
to God—though I controlled my emotions as we sat together
in the restaurant where we were eating breakfast.

The long-range reaction was far more significant and powerful. It caused me to evaluate my attitudes and actions.
When I've been tempted to violate the will of God in my
life—and I *am* tempted to do so, like every other Christian—
I think about my son's statement, "Dad, I want you to know I
want to be like you." That statement and his confidence in
me as a role model have brought me up short on several
occasions. For example, when I'm tempted to pick up a
pornographic magazine from a newsstand in an airport and
thumb through it, I think of my son's statement. When I'm
tempted to watch an adult movie in my motel room, which is
just a flip of a switch away from reality, I think of my son's
statement. When I'm tempted to rent a video or see a movie
that features activities and language that violate the will of
God, I think of my son's statement. It has been as if Kenton
were sitting or standing beside me—listening, observing, and

taking mental, emotional, and spiritual notes on my lifestyle.

In many respects this is the kind of heavy responsibility Paul was laying on Titus' shoulders when he wrote, "Encourage the young men to be self-controlled. In everything set them an example by doing what is good."

Integrity

"In your teaching show integrity" (Titus 2:7). In other words, don't violate with your life what you teach these young men. Live what you teach. Be honest and consistent. Don't be a hypocrite.

Let me clarify something very important. Paul is not saying we have to be perfect. My son said something else to me that morning. "Dad," he said, "I know you make mistakes. And so do I. But you're still my model."

That, of course, ministered to me as much as if not more than his initial statement. We do make mistakes. Those who work closely with me know that more than anything—especially my children. But it encourages me to know that he could see beyond my mistakes and my sins to my heart and what I really want to be.

Seriousness

Further, Paul said, "In your teaching show . . . seriousness" (vs. 7). Paul is not suggesting that we cannot laugh and joke and have a good time. God created humor. People who cannot laugh are to be pitied, because the Bible teaches that a "cheerful heart is good medicine" (Prov. 17:22).

Rather, Paul was teaching Titus that God's business is serious business. It's not all fun and games. It is not a rose garden every day. It involves eternal issues—life and death and ultimately, heaven and hell. There's no place for superficiality in our Christian lives. How easy it is say "Praise the Lord" or "Hallelujah" or "Isn't it great to be a Christian?" But I've discovered that some of these statements by Christians can be as superficial as a bubbly brook. There's no depth. For many of these people life is words—not day-to-day, gut-level Christian living.

Cautious Speech

Paul makes a third statement that helps us understand what it means to live a self-controlled life. "In your teaching show . . . soundness of speech that cannot be condemned" (vv. 7-8). Paul is emphasizing thinking before speaking. "Sound speech" is speech that reflects careful thought, knowledge, wisdom, and above all, truth. But the context makes it clear that Paul is also referring to the *way* we speak the truth. When it is communicated in love, it is very difficult to resist (Eph. 4:15). It is doubly difficult to resist this truth when a Christian first "walks his talk."

There is a very close association between what Paul was saying to Titus and what he wrote to Timothy regarding being "able to teach." He instructs Timothy how to respond to people who disagree with him and yet win their respect.

> Don't have anything to do with foolish and stupid arguments, because you know they produce quarrels. And the Lord's servant must not quarrel; instead, he must be kind to everyone, able to teach, not resentful. Those who oppose him he must gently instruct, in the hope that God will grant them repentance leading them to a knowledge of the truth, and that they will come to their senses and escape from the trap of the devil, who has taken them captive to do his will. (2 Tim. 2:23-26)

A gentleman calls me rather frequently on my "Let's Talk" open-line radio show on Saturdays. Dick identifies himself openly as a humanist. He's a leader in the Unitarian Church in Richardson, Texas. On one occasion my guest pastor and I had just prayed for some tornado victims in Sweetwater,

Texas. Dick called to let us know it always boggles his mind that people actually believe that they can pray about situations that involve nature and expect God to change the situation. My response was that it boggles my mind too that I can believe in a God who does control nature and can change it if He so desires. But I also reminded him that we were actually praying that God would help and comfort these people who were victims of a tornado that had actually passed through that area.

"Oh," he hurriedly said, "that's fine. I certainly wouldn't discourage that." Since he is a humanist who claims to be concerned for people, he of course would have difficulty disparaging our prayers for people who were hurting. He went on to ask me, however, if I ever considered the possibility that God and nature are one. My response was that I wasn't surprised at his question, since I knew that he was a humanist. "In actuality," I responded, "you're a pantheist." (Pantheists believe that God and nature are one and I had conversed with him enough to know that was his position).

I then explained to Dick that I believe in a God who is separate from nature—a God who created nature and who can control it if He wants to.

"Yes," he responded, "I understand that, since you believe in a personal God and I don't."

As I reflected on that conversation, as well as previous conversations, I sensed that here was a man who was not just calling to trip me up. I really believe he is searching for answers. The challenge I face every time he calls, however, is to be self-controlled. My challenge is to avoid an argument with him, to be kind, and to gently instruct a man who opposes what I believe about the Bible, God, Jesus Christ, and the Holy Spirit. I am also challenged to do this and at the same time "show integrity, seriousness and soundness of speech that cannot be condemned." If I can maintain that kind of self-control—and sometimes it is difficult—I just might be able to teach Dick and with God's help lead him to a knowledge of the truth. But if Dick is ever going to listen to what I say and share, I need to win his respect.

Humility

Self-control is reflected in humility. Paul also made reference to self-control in his letter to the Romans. After exhorting them to "renew their minds" by no longer conforming to the world's system, he wrote, "For by the grace given me I say to every one of you: Do not think of yourself more highly than you ought, but rather think of yourself with sober judgment, in accordance with the measure of faith God has given you" (Rom. 12:3). Here the phrase *sober judgment* is translated from the same basic word that Paul used in his letter to Titus. We could actually translate it, "think of yourself with self-control." The translators of the *New American Standard Bible* use the term "sound judgment."

We need to be balanced, being firm and self-confident about what we believe and at the same time reflecting a spirit of humility. The more comfortable we are with what we believe, the easier it is to respond sensitively and lovingly to those who disagree with us.

I remember when I was working on my B.A. at a liberal arts college. It was not a Christian school in the true sense of the word, although it had once been church related. One day I got into an argument with one of the professors. He was quite calm and in control, but I was out of control. Although I believe to this day that he was wrong in his beliefs, the spirit with which I responded was not reflecting the kind of self-control Paul wrote about to Titus and Timothy. I felt threatened. At that time I was also going through a deep period of inner doubt regarding what I *really* believed. Had I been more comfortable with my own beliefs, I'm confident I wouldn't have responded the way I did.

This also leads to another important observation. Threatened feelings and an arrogant attitude often go together. I'm sure I came across as a cocky, dogmatic, and arrogant student. In reality I was a threatened young man fighting for my spiritual life. As a result, I wasn't able to communicate very effectively. I'm sure this professor, as pagan as he was, knew exactly what was going on inside me. He had encountered that phenomenon many times before.

We should be encouraged, however. These feelings are not uncommon for new and growing Christians. Even Timothy had this problem. He was easily intimidated by those who opposed him. That's why Paul wrote to him and encouraged him with the words, "For God did not give us a spirit of timidity, but a spirit of power, of love and of self-discipline," that is, of self-control. Here again Paul used a form of the Greek word *sophron.* The *King James Version* reads, "For God hath not given us the spirit of fear; but of power, and of love, and of a sound mind" (2 Tim. 1:7).

Self-control and Prayer

Self-control is necessary for an effective prayer life. Peter used this concept to emphasize the importance of prayer. "The end of all things is near. Therefore be clear minded and self-controlled so that you can pray" (1 Peter 4:7). It is difficult to pray when we are confused and out of control. In fact, if we're not careful, we're tempted to try to face the pressures of life and solve our personal problems by ourselves. We step up our human efforts rather than wait on the Lord and trust Him.

I'm not suggesting that we should fold our hands and neglect our human responsibilities. There are occasions when all the prayer in the world will not solve our problems. We can see a tornado coming, ignore the storm warnings, fall on our knees and pray for protection—and get killed. Or we can listen to the storm warnings and take precautions and be saved from a natural disaster. A mature Christian takes precautions and prays at the same time.

The point Peter is making is that we Christians can get so fearful and out of control emotionally because of the vicissitudes and struggles of life that we can't even pray effectively. This is why Paul wrote to the Philippians, "Do not be anxious about anything, but in everything, by prayer and petition, with thanksgiving, present your requests to God. And the peace of God, which transcends all understanding, will guard your hearts and your minds in Christ Jesus" (Phil. 4:6-7).

A Personal Prayer

Dear Father, I realize that there are some truths I can teach others with my words. But there are other things I can only teach by *example.* I recognize from Your Word that maintaining self-control is one of those important areas that must be taught by my total lifestyle.

Father, help me to show *integrity* in what I teach others— to live what I teach, to be honest and consistent. I realize I am not perfect, but help me to acknowledge my sins and mistakes and to ask forgiveness when I fail others—my friends, my fellow employees, my children, and my mate. Help me become more and more like Jesus Christ in all of my relationships.

Father, help me to be *serious* about life. Help me get beyond the "fun and games" level of life and develop depth in my Christian experience.

Father, help me also to speak with *caution,* particularly when I am faced with the serious issues in life. I want to "show . . . soundness of speech that cannot be condemned."

Help me to respond with *kindness* and *love,* even to those who disagree with me and who try to cause me to compromise my beliefs about You. In my firmness, help me to avoid arguments and quarrels. In essence, Father, help me to "speak the truth in love."

Father, what is perhaps most important of all, help me to

reflect *humility* through self-control. Help me not to think more highly of myself than I ought to think, but to think of myself with sober judgment.

And finally, Father, help me keep a proper focus on the circumstances of life, no matter how chaotic they may become. Help me always to wait on You and to seek Your guidance through *prayer*. And help me to also take action when I should. In short, Father, help me to maintain balance, relying on You for what only You can do and faithfully doing what I must do.

Father, help me to live a self-controlled life. I thank You that I will earn a good reputation as I do so. In Jesus' name. Amen.

CHAPTER NINE

Always Treat People Justly

"He must be ... upright." (Titus 1:8)

In October of 1982, a young black man, Lenell Geter, was sentenced to life in prison for allegedly robbing a fried chicken restaurant of $615 in Greenville, Texas. Geter was a well-respected engineer and had no police record. But fortunately, after serving 477 days in prison, he was released and eventually exonerated. Geter had been falsely accused. The reasons given for this horrible injustice were racial prejudice and shoddy police work. Those of you who may have watched the treatment of this case on "60 Minutes," which precipitated a barrage of public reaction, will remember the shameful way this case was handled.

The even greater tragedy in cases like this involve those who are guilty, but never pay the consequences. Justice Gray, of the Supreme Court, once said to a man who had appeared before him in one of the lower courts and escaped conviction on the basis of a technicality, "I know that you are guilty and you know it, and I wish you to remember that one day you will stand before a better and wiser Judge and that there you will be dealt with according to justice and not according to law."

Why these stories? They relate directly to the quality of Christian maturity discussed in this chapter—being "upright." The Greek word *dikaios* is used over 70 times in the New Testament—over 30 times in the four Gospels, 6 times in the Book of Acts and over 30 times in the epistles. It is a concept that permeates the New Testament. The word, however, is used in various ways and translated with various English words, such as, "just" and "righteous." In Titus 1:8 in the NIV, it is translated "upright."

Dikaios and Salvation

The most important way *dikaios* and related words are used is to describe what happens to a person who comes to know Jesus Christ personally. Paul states this clearly in his letter to the Romans.

> I am not ashamed of the Gospel, because it is the power of God for the salvation of everyone who believes: first for the Jew, then for the Gentile. For in the Gospel a righteousness [*dikaiosune*] from God is revealed, a righteousness that is by faith from first to last, just as it is written: "the righteous [*dikaios*] will live by faith." (Rom. 1:16-17)

Here Paul refers to what theologians call "positional righteousness." When we put our faith in Jesus Christ for salvation, God sees us as being as righteous as Christ Himself. In fact, that's the only way we could ever be saved. Jesus Christ Himself is our righteousness. As Paul wrote to the Corinthians, "It is because of Him that you are in Christ Jesus, who has become for us wisdom from God—that is, our righteousness [*dikaiosune*], holiness and redemption" (1 Cor. 1:30).

The reason for this marvelous plan is that there is not one person on earth—past, present, or future—who will ever be sufficiently righteous or just in God's sight to inherit salvation. "There is no one righteous [*dikaios*], not even one; there is no one who understands, no one who seeks God. All have turned away, they have together become worthless; there is no one who does good, not even one" (Rom. 3:10-12). Later Paul tells us the solution to this horrible problem.

> But now a righteousness [*dikaiosune*] from God, apart from the law, has been made known, to which the Law and the Prophets testify. This righteousness from God comes through faith in Jesus Christ to all who believe. There is no difference, for all have sinned and fall short of the glory of God, and are justified freely by His grace through the redemption that came by Christ Jesus. God presented Him as a sacrifice of atonement, through faith in His blood. He did this to demonstrate His justice. (3:21-26)

Righteousness or *uprightness* or *justice* (whichever word you want to choose) is used over 20 times in the first five chapters alone of the Book of Romans. This represents the foundational way the Holy Spirit used this word. Paul did not mean the same thing when he used this word in his letter to Titus, but this meaning is basic to an understanding of what he did mean.

Dikaios and a Christian's Behavior

There is a second way the Holy Spirit used the word *dikaios.* In a broader sense, it means to live an upright, righteous, just, and holy life. It means to obey God and keep His commandments. Once we are made righteous through Christ by faith, we then reflect Christ's righteous life. This is what Paul meant when he wrote to the Ephesians, "For you were once darkness, but now you are light in the Lord. Live as children of light (for the fruit of the light consists in all goodness, righteousness and truth) and find out what pleases the Lord"

(Eph. 5:8-10). Earlier in the same letter Paul put it all together.

> For it is by grace you have been saved, through faith—and this not from yourselves, it is the gift of God—not by works, so that no one can boast. For we are God's workmanship, created in Christ Jesus to do good works, which God prepared in advance for us to do. (2:8-10)

This is one of the most critical distinctions in Christian theology. It is perhaps the one that Satan has used most frequently to confuse people through the centuries, in spite of the fact that it is one of the clearest teachings in Scripture. There is one major doctrinal error that runs through every major religion in the world, including the offshoots of Christianity that we call "cults" and "isms." That error is that a person can be saved by works, or that a person can be saved by a mixture of faith and works, or that a person can be saved by faith and keeps himself safe by works.

On the other side of the spectrum is another doctrinal error—the idea that a person is saved by a faith (a superficial belief) that doesn't have to produce any works. James writes, "Faith by itself, if it is not accompanied by action, is dead" (James 2:17). It is a dead faith. It is not true, saving faith, for saving faith will eventually produce the works of righteousness God planned for our lives. The extent to which we do these works, however, still depends on our commitment to Jesus Christ and our desire to do His will.

A Christian, a person who has been made righteous by faith, should also live an *upright* life, one that reflects the righteousness of Jesus Christ. The result will be a good reputation. This is what Paul's guidelines for being above reproach are all about. A Christian who wants to build a good reputation will not be overbearing, quick-tempered, given to much wine, violent, and a person who pursues dishonest gain. Rather, he will be hospitable, he will love what is good, and he will be self-controlled.

Dikaios and Relationships

This brings us now to a more specific meaning for the word *dikaios*. Paul was referring to the way we treat people. A spiritual leader in the church should be fair and just in his dealings with people. This, of course, is a specific reflection of Christ's righteousness. An upright and just person is concerned about others—that they receive what is due them. From the positive side, a just and upright person does not mistreat people. On the tough side of love, if we have the authority to do so, we should not allow others to mistreat their fellow men. Mature Christians are concerned about justice.

This is why I began this chapter with the illustration about Lenell Geter and Justice Gray. Unfortunately, there is a lot of injustice in this world—a lot we can do little about, especially as it involves prominent leaders in the world. There are situations where we must wait for God to set the record straight, even in our personal lives. We must turn the matter over to the great Judge of the universe. "Do not take revenge, my friends, but leave room for God's wrath, for it is written: 'It is Mine to avenge; I will repay,' says the Lord" (Rom. 12:19).

But there is a realm in which we all operate as Christians where we can practice justice and be upright in our dealings with our fellow human beings, especially those in our immediate family, our fellow Christians, and non-Christians with whom we associate on a regular basis.

Over the years, I have seen Christians hurt—desperately hurt—because of self-centered, insensitive, and hard-hearted Christians. One of the saddest comments I've heard over the years from believers is that they would rather do business with non-Christians than with Christians because Christians, they say, are more unfair, irresponsible, and in some cases, more ruthless than non-Christians.

I realize, as most people do, that one bad experience with a Christian can cause someone to generalize about every Christian under the sun, and that's unfortunate. Frankly, that's not been my experience. Dealing with Christians has been a very positive experience for me. But it is still true that there are some believers who bring shame to the name of Jesus Christ because of their lack of justice and fairness in dealing with people. This is a two-way street: there are people who take advantage of other Christians because for some strange reason they believe that Christians in business owe them a better deal simply because they are Christians, and there are Christian employers who demand more from Christian employees simply because those employees are Christians. Both approaches are unjust.

Being unfair to people, particularly when we are in positions of authority, has been a problem ever since sin entered the world. This is why Moses was advised to "select capable men . . . who fear God, trustworthy men who hate dishonest gain" to help him rule Israel (Ex. 18:21).

This is also why Paul wrote to the Colossians, "Masters, provide your slaves with what is right [*dikaios*] and fair, because you know that you also have a Master in heaven" (Col. 4:1) and told husbands to love their wives just as Christ loved the church, giving Himself up for us (Eph. 5:25). Peter was even more specific when he said, "Husbands, in the same way be considerate as you live with your wives, and treat them with respect as the weaker partner and heirs with you of the gracious gift of life, so that nothing will hinder your prayers" (1 Peter 3:7).

The Example of Joseph

As I was preparing this chapter, I was particularly impressed with Joseph, Mary's husband. You know the story. "Mary was pledged to be married to Joseph, but before they came together, she was found to be with child through the Holy Spirit" (Matt. 1:18). Joseph found himself in an embarrassing predicament. He was engaged—not legally married—and his wife-to-be was pregnant. Tongues were wagging. How in the world do you explain this kind of situation? Humanly speaking, there was only one way. They had had sexual relations before they were married, which was a violation of the Law of God. Can't you just hear the conversations?

A friend: "Joseph, what's with you and Mary? You're in big trouble, my friend. People are talking all over town."

A priest: "Joseph, you rascal! You *are* in big trouble. I want to see you in my office first thing in the morning. You know better than to take advantage of Mary. Furthermore, you've brought disgrace on all of us in Israel."

The parents: "You two ought to be ashamed of yourselves! What do you think we've taught you all these years? What are people going to think of us?"

Joseph and Mary: "You're really not going to believe this, but..."

Responses: "Incredible! We've heard of rationalizations before, but this is one of the biggest and boldest we've heard yet! An angel appeared? Angels are sexless! The Holy Spirit? Well, the Holy Spirit only came upon great people like David and some of the other outstanding prophets. You're both crazy if you think you can get by with this one!"

Note how Joseph responded. "Because Joseph her husband was a righteous man [*dikaios*] and did not want to expose her to public disgrace, he had in mind to divorce her quietly" (Matt. 1:19). If we look casually at Joseph's response, we might conclude he was simply embarrassed and trying to save his own reputation. Not so! He was concerned for Mary because he was a just man. He understood her plight and the price she was paying to be the mother of the Son of God. He didn't want to expose her to public disgrace.

Mercifully, of course, God stepped in and reassured Joseph that their predicament and humiliation were only temporary (Matt. 1:20-21). The pain they would have to bear that was caused by those who were critical because of their ignorance, insensitivity, and unbelief would be well worth it when the angels sang from heaven, "Glory to God in the highest, and on earth peace to men on whom His favor rests" (Luke 2:14). And when the wise men from the East would later bring gifts, lay them at the feet of Jesus, and recognize Him as a King, it would be worth it all!

May God give us more men like Joseph—upright, just men who are willing to put their own egos behind them and be concerned for others. How many men do you know who have gotten women pregnant out of wedlock and then left them high and dry to bear the burden that resulted from a moment of lust and self-indulgence? Of course, I am not putting all the blame on men. This kind of sin is a two-way street. But how easy it is to take advantage of someone else and then allow that person to struggle through the problem all alone! That's the ultimate in unjust behavior.

The Fallen and Hurting Christian

And then there are those Christians who fail God and who are shunned by the Christian community. On one occasion a former student of mine stopped by the office unannounced. It was one of those hectic days. I'd been up since 3:30 in the morning working on a project. When he arrived, I was just completing a rather heavy meeting in the middle of the afternoon and was about to "crash" and call it quits for the day. Frankly, I didn't feel like seeing anyone, let alone talking.

Somehow, however, the Holy Spirit quieted my heart. Recognizing him immediately, I invited him into my office. He apologized for dropping in unannounced.

After some small talk, he began to unload a very sad story, one he said he had not intended to tell. Let me succinctly share his story. After graduation from the school where I taught, he married a girl who was also one of my students. He became a pastor. From the beginning his marriage was in trouble. I realize I heard only one side of the story, but I think I heard enough and knew enough of the principals involved to conclude that his report was fairly accurate. His wife became a thorn in his side—a millstone around his neck. She was always hurting other people's feelings in his congregation, creating divisions, gossiping, and keeping his own family in a state of confusion. His life as a pastor was filled with embarrassment and heartache. After a number of years, he became so frustrated that he gave up. In anger and resentment, he divorced her and left the ministry.

When he arrived in my office that day, he had been wandering in the wilderness for nearly three years. He acknowledged that he had sinned during that time, becoming involved with another woman. In recent months he had broken off the relationship because he knew it was wrong. He felt helpless, frustrated, and rejected by even his closest friends. Even the people in the church he had built his life into for years had dropped him like a hot potato, even though they knew his life had been a living hell. No one reached out to help him.

One day he had stopped to see another pastor he knew well. The pastor was just concluding a counseling session and his secretary called him on the intercom telling him who was waiting. The pastor responded by saying he was too busy—too busy even to step out of his office and say hello to a man he knew was hurting.

At that moment in my office this big hulk of a man broke down and wept. He wasn't justifying himself. He acknowledged his anger and his bitterness. He acknowledged his guilt over the fact that he had finally given up and divorced his wife and left the ministry—even though he had been advised by four well-known pastors that he probably didn't have any choice. "But, Gene," he said, "the man wouldn't even say hello to me!"

I had almost done the same thing that afternoon. Thank God, the Holy Spirit didn't let me do it, as tired as I was. I sat and listened to his story for over two hours. My heart went out to him in his pain.

After listening, I suggested biblical steps for getting his life back in order and in harmony with the will of God. He listened. "I want to help you out," I said. "My time is limited, but I want to help."

I'll never forget his response. He looked down and tried to fight the tears. "Gene, what you just said means more to me than anything I've heard for the last three years. Though I may never bother you again and though I may not take your advice totally, I know you care and right now I just need a friend who will listen."

I would be dishonest if I told you it was easy in that situation to be just and upright and caring. It's impossible for me to talk with everyone who wants to share his burdens. If I tried, I'd probably end up in desperate straights myself. But I do thank God I didn't let that one pass me by. Being upright is indeed a route to earning respect in the eyes of others.

CHAPTER TEN

Avoid the Peril of the Pendulum

"He must be . . . holy." (Titus 1:8)

Several years ago my wife and I visited Guatemala. One experience left a marked impression on my life. In one small village one of the missionaries drew our attention to a church with a large series of steps leading up to a large courtyard. We then noticed people crawling on their hands and knees up the concrete steps through the courtyard and then into the church. Periodically people went through this routine, even though their knees would eventually bleed as they crawled the hundreds of yards over the rough concrete surface.

What would cause people to engage in this kind of religious ritual? The answer is relatively simple. They believe that this is one way they can be forgiven of their sins and become holy.

This real-life story introduces us to the next quality of maturity listed by Paul in his letter to Titus. Christians are to be holy. But what is holiness? How do you become holy? How do you maintain holiness?

The concept of holiness is a prevalent theme in both the Old and New Testaments. The Scriptures are clear! Speaking to the Children of Israel, God said, "Be holy because I, the Lord your God, am holy" (Lev. 19:2). In the New Testament Peter emphasized the same commandment. "But just as He who called you is holy, so be holy in all you do; for it is written: 'Be holy, because I am holy' " (1 Peter 1:15-16). The word *holy*, in relationship both to the character of God and how we are to imitate that character, is repeated hundreds of times in the Bible.

New Testament Synonyms

New Testament writers used several words to make the point that Christians are to live holy lives. There are at least three Greek words that can be classified as synonyms. The word used most frequently is *hagios*. Almost without exception this word is translated into English with the word "holy."

New Testament writers also used a second word—*hosios*. Though this word is not used as frequently as *hagios*, it is also translated with the English word "holy." The third word is *hagnos*. Though this word is considered a synonym, it is usually translated with the English words "pure" or "chaste."

The Greek word that Paul used in writing to Titus to describe an aspect of Christian maturity is *hosios*. Paul used this same word when he wrote to Timothy and said, "I want men everywhere to lift up holy hands in prayer, without anger or disputing" (1 Tim. 2:8). He also used this word when he wrote to the Thessalonians, reminding them of the way in which he and his coworkers lived among these people. "You are witnesses, and so is God, of how holy, righteous and blameless we were among you who believe" (1 Thes. 2:10).

This brings us back to our initial questions. What is holiness? How do we become holy? And how can we maintain this holiness?

Before we look at the answers to these questions, we need to look at some misconceptions regarding the answers to these questions. Even though this concept is used so frequently throughout the Bible, there are few subjects that have created more confusion in the minds of Christians over the years.

In this chapter, we'll look at what holiness is not, and in our next chapter we'll discuss what holiness is.

Some Misconceptions

I want to preface my remarks by stating that I am not questioning the sincerity of the people who hold some of these viewpoints. In fact, I did not at all question the sincerity of those people who were crawling hundreds of yards over rough concrete in that little village in Guatemala. They were desperately seeking to be forgiven for their sins. Perhaps the most simple and practical definition of holiness is to be "without sin." That is the statement that was made about the Lord Jesus Christ while He lived His life on earth. We read, "For we do not have a High Priest who is unable to sympathize with our weaknesses, but we have One who has been tempted in every way, just as we are—yet was without sin" (Heb. 4:15).

Furthermore, as I deal with those misconceptions, I am not condemning these people. That is not my prerogative. Also, I realize there may be people reading this book who hold to some of the views I am going to define as misconceptions. That in no way means that I love or respect them less. I simply want to share what I've observed from personal experience through the years, and from my own personal study of Scripture and the writings of those who have studied the Scriptures even more extensively than I have.

Perfectionism. Some Christians believe they can actually live a life so much like Christ that they can reach a state of perfection and sinlessness. I once attended and spoke at a "holiness convention" where this very doctrine was being taught from the platform. Though I heard a number of people speak at that time and met a lot of wonderful people who were simply attending the convention, my personal opinion is that I didn't hear anyone or meet anyone who was totally free from sinful thoughts, attitudes, and actions—including myself.

Please don't misunderstand. I'm not questioning the sincerity of these Christians. I probably never met more devoted Christians. And I am not suggesting I had opportunity to draw these conclusions from personal observations of their lives. My conclusions are based on what I feel the Bible teaches, that is, that it is impossible for any Christian to live a perfect life that is totally and consistently free from sin. The Apostle John wrote, "If we claim to be without sin, we deceive ourselves and the truth is not in us" (1 John 1:8). Even the Apostle Paul stated regarding his own life,

> Not that I have already obtained all this, or have already been made perfect, but I press on to take hold of that for which Christ Jesus took hold of me. Brothers, I do not consider myself yet to have taken hold of it. But one thing I do: Forgetting what is behind and straining toward what is ahead, I press on toward the goal to win the prize for which God has called me heavenward in Christ Jesus. (Phil. 3:12-14)

To be fair, of course, it is important to note that most of these people would not say they *cannot* sin. Rather, they believe they have reached a state in their Christian lives enabling them, through God's grace and power, to keep from sinning in any way. Again, I would have to disagree, not only on the basis of what Scripture teaches, but from a purely pragmatic point of view. When I meet a husband, for example, who claims to be free from sin, it makes me wish I could spend some time talking with his wife. If she would be perfectly honest with me, I am convinced I would soon discover the truth about her husband's claims. He's far from perfect—especially when measured against the life of Jesus Christ. The same, of course, would be true of a wife who claims to be totally free from sin. I'm confident her husband could shed some light on the subject.

Asceticism. There have been other theological positions throughout Christian history that promote ways to become holy. For example, there are people who choose to live ascetic lives. During the fourth century particularly, hundreds of people sought to escape temptation by punishing their bodies and by living as hermits. The extremes to which they went in their attempts to deny gratification of "physical lusts" are incredible. Saint Esemius wore so many chains that he had to crawl around on his hands and knees. Beserian, a monk, would not even give in to his body's desire for rest or sleep. For forty years he would not lie down while sleeping. Others lived in caves, dens of beasts, dry wells, and even tombs. To suffer this discomfort was considered to be beneficial and a sign of victory over the body. To them, it was a means of becoming holy.

Again, there is absolutely no basis in Scripture for this kind of approach to obtaining and maintaining holiness. In actuality, this approach to the Christian life resulted to a great degree from a syncretization of Greek philosophy with Christian theology. Many of the Greek philosophers taught that the body was evil and the spirit was good. Because our bodies do give us a lot of problems that lead us into sinful actions, it was relatively easy for Christians to adopt this thinking into their point of view.

Over the years there have been those who believed ascetic practice was the way to holiness, but have not gone to such extremes. For example, there are those yet today who take vows of chastity and poverty, giving up the right to be married and to own any material possessions. They believe this will make them more holy in God's sight.

This approach to the Christian life is very interesting in view of the fact that Paul identified this kind of lifestyle in the New Testament world as being motivated by evil spirits (1 Tim. 4:1).

> Such teachings come through hypocritical liars, whose consciences have been seared as with a hot iron. They forbid people to marry and order them to abstain from certain foods, which God created to be received with thanksgiving by those who believe and know the truth. For everything God created is good, and nothing is to be rejected if it is received with thanksgiving, because it is consecrated by the Word of God and prayer. (1 Tim. 4:2-5)

Abstaining from legitimate sexual relations is not a sign of or a means to holiness. Vows of chastity have led to some of the worst forms of sexual immorality. The reason this happens is that it is against God's created plan for us. God created men and women, generally speaking, to live together in a sacred relationship we call marriage. There are those, of course, who willingly choose a single life and seem to be particularly gifted in this way. Being unmarried does not create a problem morally. But this is not the normal state of things, and to promote this as a way of holiness can lead to great temptation and ultimately to sin.

Interestingly, Paul stated only one reason for married people to abstain from sexual relations. Writing to the Corinthians, he said, "Do not deprive each other except by mutual consent and for a time, so that you may devote yourselves to prayer. Then come together again so that Satan will not tempt you because of your lack of self-control" (1 Cor. 7:5).

Here Paul is teaching that God designed the marital relationship as one means to remain holy and pure. Incidentally, one of the reasons Paul had to say this to the Corinthians is that they had so perverted sex in their pagan state that it was difficult to develop a proper view of this relationship when they became Christians.

Legalism. Through the years there have also been Christians who believed they could become holy by following a set of rules. This is particularly evident among a lot of Bible-believing Christians today. Their emphasis is on externals—what you wear, how you fix your hair, what you don't do, and so on. I grew up in this kind of religious community. Wearing rings was considered worldly and sinful—even wedding rings. Lipstick was a sign of sin and certain hairstyles were considered evil.

And yet I noticed, even as a young Christian, that these people often reflected jealousy and pride. They were judgmental and prejudiced. They gossiped about one another and were often bitter. In essence they overlooked those internal qualities that are so important to true holiness.

I also noticed that even though they believed wearing rings was sinful, the women would wear some of the most expensive and beautiful diamond brooches available. This kind of thinking usually leads to inconsistency and compensation. When we go to extremes in one area, we usually make up for it in another area.

The women were also taught to wear coverings on their heads when they came to church. This was to be a sign of humility. However, I noticed two things. The older women particularly purchased some of the most beautiful veils they could find. They were exquisite. In fact, some seemed to see which one could wear the most beautiful veil.

The younger women often responded differently. Many would wear the smallest strips across their heads that they could find and still have it considered a covering. Legalism, you see, always leads to some way to circumvent an extrabiblical rule or requirement.

This is exactly what the Pharisees did on many occasions.

They set up legalistic rules and then planned ways to circumvent those rules. For example, Jesus confronted this behavior on one occasion. He said to the Pharisees,

> You have a fine way of setting aside the commands of God in order to observe your own traditions! For Moses said, "Honor your father and mother," and, "Anyone who curses his father or mother must be put to death." But you say that if a man says to his father or mother: "Whatever help you might otherwise have received from me is Corban" (that is, a gift devoted to God), then you no longer let him do anything for his father or mother. Thus you nullify the Word of God by your tradition that you have handed down. And you do many things like that. (Mark 7:9-13)

In essence, the Pharisees did not want to help their parents. Consequently, they came up with a plan to simply designate their money as a gift devoted to God. They were then free from their responsibility. In addition, they came up with all kinds of ways to spend the money on themselves and still consider it a gift to God and to set their consciences free from caring for their parents. Jesus said that was hypocrisy.

Coming closer to home, there are Christians who believe the degree of holiness they attain is directly related to the amount of time they spend in prayer, Bible study, and other forms of religious exercise. This too is a form of legalism. Many of these people have been well-meaning ministers and missionaries—people who have been classified as mystics. They are able to spend hours and hours in prayer and meditation due to their chosen vocation. This, they believe, is a means to holiness.

It needs to be noted that if holiness can only be obtained and maintained by spending hours in the presence of God, this would mean that ordinary Christians who have to go to work every day, who have to spend time caring for their families and facing other demands in life cannot be as holy as those who spend hours in prayer and meditation.

Again, of course, we have seen an overreaction to this kind of legalism. We have gone to the other extreme and neglected these important aspects of the Christian life. Prayer and Bible study *are* essential to Christian growth and maturity. In fact, I have just completed a very extensive time log study. I recorded all of my activities for a period of two weeks, actually covering fifteen days. I recorded my activities from the time I got up in the morning until I retired at night. I then analyzed all these activities and the amount of time I was spending doing various things. Frankly, I was embarrassed by the small amount of time that I spend alone with God in prayer and personal meditation. True, I spent a number of hours studying the Word of God to prepare messages, but I do not feel that this should become a complete substitute for nurturing my own *personal* relationship with God. What I learned in that study has caused me to set new goals for my own life.

The Results of These Misconceptions

With any emphasis that is not based on Scripture come unfortunate results. For example, those who teach *perfectionism* often create horrible guilt in people who fail. And people will fail! Or it causes people to rationalize their sinful attitudes and actions as being unsinful—which is a form of self-deception—and that, of course, is sin in itself. For others, a perfectionistic approach to the Christian life causes them to give up, feeling they have failed God and there is no real hope. Some even believe they have committed the unpardonable sin—a tragic point of view indeed!

Asceticism causes Christians to remove themselves from the world and concentrate on themselves. This is a direct contradiction to what Jesus taught. We are to be "the light of the world." We are to let our "light shine before men, that they may see [our] good deeds and praise [our] Father in heaven" (Matt. 5:14-16). Paul states that we are to be in the world, but not part of the world (1 Cor. 5:9-10). In other words, it is possible to live in this world and still live a holy life. In fact, that is one of the reasons God has left us on earth—to communicate His holiness to those who do not know God.

An emphasis on *legalism* has also created some unfortunate results. Some Christians have overreacted to this kind of teaching and gone to the other extreme. They move from *legalism* to *license*. There *are* things that Christians should not do and places we should not go and things we should not see—simply because they do involve sinful attitudes and actions. But to put an emphasis on *externals* and to neglect the *internal* qualities of Christianity will normally lead to legalism and a false view of holiness.

What then is the answer to our questions? What is true holiness and how do we attain and maintain it? That's another chapter. I hope that against the backdrop of these misconceptions we can more easily grasp a true biblical perspective on the subject.

Here are some general principles to help us avoid these misconceptions.

- Interpreting Scripture out of context always leads to misconceptions.
- Extreme points of view are usually not accurate biblical perspectives.
- Extreme points of view do not create positive results.
- A true biblical perspective coincides with reality.
- True holiness is attractive, not repulsive.

This final point is particularly important. People are generally attracted to true holiness. They like what they see and respect people who reflect godly lifestyles. This is often true even though they may not accept that way of life personally.

Conversely, many people are repulsed by a false concept of holiness. It is not attractive. It does not function as "salt"—making people thirsty for more.

What then is true holiness? Let's move to our next chapter.

CHAPTER ELEVEN

Seek to Reflect God's Character

"He must be ... holy." (Titus 1:8)

As we noted in chapter 10, there are three basic Greek words that convey the idea of holiness in the New Testament: *hagios, hosios,* and *hagnos.* Together, these words and their various forms (which are translated "holiness," "hallowed," "sanctified," "purified," etc.) are used approximately 300 times in the New Testament.

Although Paul used the word *hosios* in his letter to Titus, the most common word for "holy" is *hagios,* which is used in its various forms approximately 265 times. Holiness does indeed receive very strong emphasis in the New Testament. This should not surprise us in view of who God is and the fact that He wants us to be holy because He is holy (1 Peter 1:16).

A Biblical Principle of Interpretation

In order to understand holiness and how to live a holy life, we need to look carefully at the letters written to the New Testament churches and to those who were responsible to guide these new and growing bodies of believers—men such as Titus and Timothy. Our primary source for this series of studies, of course, is the letter that Paul wrote to Titus. And in that letter Paul told Titus to instruct the people to be holy.

We must not, of course, ignore teachings regarding holiness in the Gospels and the Book of Acts. However, we must not develop our view of how to live a holy life solely from these sections of the New Testament. The reason for this principle of interpretation is that the Gospels record the activities of Jesus Christ in laying the foundations for the church. In the Book of Acts, Luke records the activities of the apostles and other key New Testament leaders in launching local churches. But the New Testament letters give specific instructions on how to live the Christian life.

We must look at the section of Scripture that is designed by the Holy Spirit to teach us basic truth regarding how to live the Christian life. We must then interpret the other two sections of Scripture in view of what is taught in the letters.

To ignore this principle of interpretation leads to serious misconceptions. In addition to those we looked at in our last chapter on being holy (perfectionism, asceticism, and legalism), it has led some Christians to more specific misinterpretations that are very current in the Christian world.

Before we look at some of these current misconceptions and then at what I believe is a correct biblical interpretation of holiness, let me once again state that I am not questioning the sincerity of the majority of those who hold to one or more of these views. If you are among them, it doesn't mean you're not living a holy life. It may mean, however, that you are struggling with some confusion in your Christian experience.

Some Current Misconceptions

Some people believe that the answers to the questions on how to become holy and maintain that holiness are contained primarily in the Book of Acts. This is the *first* misconception. Holding to this principle of interpretation is similar to suggesting that the Children of Israel, once they were in the Promised Land, should have tried to duplicate in their experience what had happened at Mt. Sinai when God revealed Himself and gave His holy commandments. "There was thunder and lightning, with a thick cloud over the mountain, and a very loud trumpet blast. Everyone in the camp trembled. . . . The Lord descended on it in fire. The smoke billowed up from it like smoke from a furnace, the whole mountain trembled violently, and the sound of the trumpet grew louder and louder. Then Moses spoke and the voice of God answered him" (Ex. 19:16-19). Because of God's presence, the Children of Israel were not able to go near the mountain. If they did, they were to be put to death (19:12). There is no question that this phenomenon was very spectacular and was never repeated again in Israel.

Just so, when Jesus Christ launched the church, He did so with even more unusual events. The coming of the Holy Spirit was accompanied by "signs, wonders and various miracles, and gifts of the Holy Spirit" distributed according to the will of God (Heb. 2:4). The major difference between Mt. Sinai and God's New Testament revelation is that God used more people to reveal His New Covenant. It began with His own Son, Jesus Christ, whose deity was confirmed by these "miraculous signs" (John 20:30-31). The revelation continued through the select group of men called apostles. Their message was also verified by signs, wonders, and miracles. In fact, these were the signs that marked true apostles (2 Cor. 12:12). God also worked through other New Testament Christians who were uniquely recognized as being anointed by the Holy Spirit in a special way to help launch His church—men like Barnabas, Stephen, Philip, and others.

Furthermore, this New Testament revelation happened over a long period of time and in more than one geographical area. And most importantly, this message was not primarily for Israel, as it was at Mt. Sinai. It was for the whole world, including both Jews and Gentiles.

It is in the Book of Acts that Luke records the special events in history surrounding the launching of the church. To attempt to duplicate the events and experiences during this time can lead to false conclusions, particularly in the area of how to live a holy life.

A *second* mistake is to believe that we cannot become holy as God intends without a "second work of grace"—a special experience that usually occurs some time after we are converted to Jesus Christ.

This view also has its roots in events recorded in the Book of Acts. These include the experience at Pentecost when the Holy Spirit came upon those waiting in the Upper Room (Acts 2:1-13) and the experience of Jerusalem Christians following Peter's release from prison and the believers' prayer for God to stretch out His hand "to heal and perform miraculous signs and wonders" (Acts 4:30). We read that "after they prayed, the place where they were meeting was shaken. And they were all filled with the Holy Spirit and spoke the Word of God boldly" (Acts 4:31). Other powerful experiences were those of Cornelius and his household (Acts 10:44-48) and the Ephesians after Paul's arrival there (19:1-7).

A *third* misconception is that we cannot have this experience which gives us a new level of spirituality and holiness without waiting on God and pleading with Him to give it. This has led some Christians to coin the phrase "praying through." Again, much of this doctrine comes from the occasion in the Book of Acts when Jesus told His small band of followers to wait in Jerusalem for the Holy Spirit to come (Acts 1:4). Waiting in Jerusalem, they "all joined together constantly in prayer" (1:14), and while they were waiting and praying, the Holy Spirit came.

I remember that when I was a student at Moody Bible

Institute, several leaders on campus started holding all-night prayer meetings. The primary purpose was to wait on God and seek a special experience that would enable us to be more holy and spiritual. Being a young and uninformed Christian, I didn't want to miss anything special that God had for me. I couldn't sleep one night, so I got up and went to this all-night prayer session. When I arrived, I heard students stand up and share that the Holy Spirit wouldn't let them sleep and they had to get up and come. I felt I had to get up and say the same thing.

In retrospect, I recognize that I was imitating the others, though I was very sincere at the time. I doubt very much that the Holy Spirit had anything to do with my not sleeping. I just didn't want to miss out on something. It also sounded very spiritual to stand up and testify regarding the Holy Spirit's work in my life.

I am not opposed to all-night prayer meetings, and I do believe the Holy Spirit works in special ways when people pray. But I am convinced now that the purpose for these meetings was not biblical. The school administration soon became convinced of that and terminated the meetings. Students were getting confused, and it was creating a division on campus. For example, some of those who attended these meetings looked down on students who didn't. You see, what is of the Holy Spirit does not create spiritual pride, but humility. We were violating some very important biblical principles. God never instructs us to seek holiness in this way.

The *fourth* misconception is that the sign that we have achieved this new level of spirituality and holiness is speaking in tongues. In the Book of Acts, frequently when people gathered and were "filled with the Holy Spirit," they *did* speak in tongues. The major problem with this view is that Paul's letter to the Corinthians clearly demonstrates that there is no correlation between holiness and speaking in tongues. In fact, the Corinthians were the most carnal and worldly church described in the New Testament. After telling them that they did "not lack any spiritual gift" (1 Cor. 1:7) in the church, Paul proceeded to alert them to the fact that he could not write to them as "spiritual, but as worldly—mere infants in Christ" (3:1).

On one occasion I spoke at a convention attended by both charismatic and non-charismatic Christians. One of my messages was based on Paul's first letter to the Corinthians, in which I demonstrated in great detail the very point I've just made, that spirituality and speaking in tongues were not related. Following my message, several pastors who serve charismatic churches asked to drive me to my motel. They wanted to chat with me further.

Frankly, I didn't know what I was getting into. On the way they surprised me with a very positive statement. "Gene," one pastor said, "we don't agree with you in everything you taught this morning, but frankly, this was the first time that we've seen clearly that Paul's letter to the Corinthians and particularly what he said about the charismatic gifts was an indictment of them because of their worldliness." I appreciated their response and their sensitivity to me. They were true Christian gentlemen, though it was true I didn't agree with their position on tongues speaking. But we did agree that there was no correlation in the Corinthian church between spirituality and the fact that these Christians spoke in tongues.

All of these misconceptions relate to the fact that a view of holiness and how to obtain and maintain it has been developed from various experiences described primarily in the Book of Acts. The focus of this interpretation is on what is recorded in the Book of Acts and what is written in the Gospels. Furthermore, what is written in the New Testament letters particularly is treated as peripheral, rather than as central, as I believe it should be treated.

A Biblical Perspective

Against this backdrop, let's look at what the Bible says about holiness. *First,* all Christians are perfectly holy in God's sight in terms of position in Christ. All believers are identified as "saints" in the New Testament; the basic word *hagios* is translated "saints" approximately 60 times. Even the Corinthians—as sinful and carnal as they were—were called "saints" or those who were "sanctified in Christ Jesus" (1 Cor. 1:2). Literally, Paul was calling these people "holy ones" in spite of their worldly lifestyles.

Paul underscored this reality in his letter to the Colossians when he identified them all "as God's chosen people, holy and dearly loved" (Col. 3:12). God, therefore, sees us as already perfect because of His perfect Son, Jesus Christ. If this were not true, no one could be saved. Theologians often call this great doctrinal truth "positional sanctification." In the mind of God, in Christ we are already set apart as His holy people. This happens the moment we put our faith in Christ and are saved.

Second, becoming holy and Christlike in a practical sense is a progressive process that will continue until we are with Jesus Christ in heaven. This is the great emphasis in the New Testament letters. Again and again, we are instructed to become like Christ in His holiness. Paul's prayer for the Thessalonians summarizes God's plan for believers of all time. "May God Himself, the God of peace, sanctify you through and through. May your whole spirit, soul and body be kept blameless at the coming of our Lord Jesus Christ" (1 Thes. 5:23). Theologians often identify this process as "progressive sanctification."

Third, becoming holy as God intended involves an act of the will following our conversion to Jesus Christ. This is the thrust of many New Testament letters, particularly after the Holy Spirit inspired the authors of these letters to explain our position in Christ. Paul's letters to the Ephesians and

Romans most clearly illustrate this emphasis. For example, in the first three chapters of Ephesians, Paul outlines their *position* in Christ. In the last three chapters, he instructs believers to *become like Christ*—"to live a life worthy of the calling" they have received (Eph. 4:1).

We see the same pattern in the letter to the Romans. The first eleven chapters outline in great detail our position in Christ. The remaining chapters describe how we are to live a holy life in view of our position in Christ.

For an example, look at Paul's words as he made this transition in Romans 12. He wrote, "I urge you . . . to offer your bodies as living sacrifices, holy and pleasing to God— which is your spiritual worship" (Rom. 12:1). This step involves an act of the will after conversion to Christ. Paul was writing to Christians in Rome; he calls them "brothers."

As a Christian, have you offered your body to Christ as a living sacrifice? Writing to the Corinthians, many of whom were living immoral lives, Paul asks them this pointed question: "Do you not know that your body is a temple of the Holy Spirit, who is in you, whom you have received from God? You are not your own; you were bought at a price. Therefore honor God with your body" (1 Cor. 6:19-20).

Fourth, the degree to which we live holy lives depends on the extent to which we keep in step with the Holy Spirit and His plan for our lives. It is not insignificant that the word *hagios* is used approximately ninety times to identify God's spirit as "holy." Writing to the Galatians, Paul made this point very specific. "So I say, live by the Spirit, and you will not gratify the desires of the sinful nature. For the sinful nature desires what is contrary to the Spirit, and the Spirit what is contrary to the sinful nature" (Gal. 5:16-17).

It is clear that every Christian has a choice. Either we're going to "keep in step with the Spirit" (Gal. 5:25) and do what He desires, or we will keep in step with the sinful nature and do what we desire.

Fifth, a Christian who lives by the Spirit reflects the "fruit of the Spirit" rather than the "acts of the sinful nature." In Galatians 5, Paul outlines the fruit of the Holy Spirit, a true reflection of holiness, and contrasts this "fruit" with the "acts of the sinful nature . . . sexual immorality, impurity and debauchery; idolatry and witchcraft; hatred, discord, jealousy, fits of rage, selfish ambition, dissensions, factions and envy; drunkenness, orgies, and the like" (Gal. 5:19-21). On the other hand, "the fruit of the Spirit is love, joy, peace, patience, kindness, goodness, faithfulness, gentleness and self-control" (5:22-23).

Sixth, the primary resource that enables us to "keep in step with the Spirit" is the Word of God. The Holy Spirit is the author of Scripture. Men like Paul and Peter and John "spoke from God as they were carried along by the Holy Spirit" (2 Peter 1:21). Jesus told the apostles this would happen. Alone with His eleven men in the Upper Room (Judas had already left), Jesus said, "I have much more to say to you, more than you can now bear. But when He, the Spirit of truth, comes, He will guide you into all truth" (John 16:12). That is exactly what happened. Initially these men spoke the Word directly as it was revealed. Later the Holy Spirit led them to write it down, which resulted in what we call the New Testament. Writing to the Colossians, Paul wrote, "Let the Word of Christ dwell in you richly as you teach and admonish one another with all wisdom, and as you sing psalms, hymns and spiritual songs with gratitude in your hearts to God" (Col. 3:16). Since the Holy Spirit is the divine author of Scripture, and since He dwells in every believer, in some miraculous way, as we yield our lives to Him, He will enable us to live out these truths in our lives, to cause the written Word to reflect the living Word—Jesus Christ Himself.

Seventh, this process of becoming holy is uniquely linked with how we use our minds. This is why Paul followed his statement in Romans 12:1 in which he encouraged these Christians to offer their bodies as living, holy sacrifices to God with these words: "Do not conform any longer to the pattern of this world, but be transformed by the renewing of your mind. Then you will be able to test and prove what God's will is—His good, pleasing and perfect will" (Rom. 12:2).

How we use our minds is directly related to whether we live a holy life. This is why Paul concluded his letter to the Philippians by saying, "Finally, brothers, whatever is true, whatever is noble, whatever is right, whatever is pure, whatever is lovely, whatever is admirable—if anything is excellent or praiseworthy—think about such things" (Phil. 4:8).

Eighth, though becoming holy is definitely a personal experience, more is said about becoming holy as a corporate experience. Out of the over 225 times *hagios* is used in the New Testament, 78 times it refers to becoming holy as a corporate body and only about 6 times to becoming holy as individual Christians.

Paul beautifully captures this truth in his letter to the Ephesians—"In Him [Christ] the whole building is joined together and rises to become a holy temple in the Lord" (Eph. 2:21). It is true that each of us has a physical body that is described as the temple of the Holy Spirit. But all of us together are a temple of the Holy Spirit. God uniquely dwells in the church, and it is the will of God that together believers reflect the fruit of the Spirit, God's holiness. That's why we need each other. That's why Paul wrote to the Ephesians, "From Him [Christ] the whole body, joined and held together by every supporting ligament, grows and builds itself up in love, as each part does its work" (Eph. 4:16).

A Final Word

When all is said and done, holiness is still an individual matter. No one else can make the important decisions for us that cause us to grow in Christ and to live a holy life.

In the Old Testament, Joseph stands out as a classic illustration of what holiness involves. You'll remember that after he was mercilessly sold into slavery by his brothers, God blessed him, and he miraculously became a servant in the household of Potiphar—a man who served Pharaoh as captain of the guard. Potiphar's wife took a liking to Joseph and tried to seduce him. Day after day she kept at him. But Joseph refused to sin against God and his master. However, one day all of the other servants were gone. This was her moment. "She caught him by his cloak and said, 'Come to bed with me!' But he left his cloak in her hand, and ran out of the house" (Gen. 39:12).

In researching the subject of holiness, I came across a very interesting paragraph in a book by Richard C. Trench entitled *Synonyms of the New Testament* (Eerdmans). After tracing the origin of the three Greek words *hagios, hosios,* and *hagnos*, he refers to Joseph as an illustration. He wrote that when Joseph was "tempted to sin by his Egyptian mistress," he "approved himself *hosios* in reverencing those everlasting sanctities of the marriage bond, which God had founded, and which he could not violate without sinning against Him." Furthermore, he pointed out that Joseph "approved himself *hagios* in that he separated himself from any unholy fellowship with his temptress." And finally, "he approved himself *hagnos* in that he kept his body pure and undefiled" (pp. 333–334).

If Joseph could live a holy life in all three dimensions before the law was given at Mt. Sinai, before Jesus Christ ever came to earth to model holiness, before the Holy Spirit came to assist us in living a holy life, and before the Word of God was revealed in its entirety, how much more should we as Christians be able to live a holy life today? We have *all* of these resources at our disposal. Insofar as we live holy lives, we will be liked and respected by others, as Joseph was.

CHAPTER TWELVE

Live a Disciplined Life

"He must be ... disciplined." (Titus 1:8)

I n the New Testament the English word *disciplined* is translated from the Greek word *egkrates*, which means having power, mastering, controlling, curbing, or restraining. In Titus 1:8, Paul is referring primarily to being self-controlled. To get a clearer picture of what Paul really means, let's look at the basic concept as it's used in other places in the New Testament.

A New Testament Situation

The idea of discipline is fleshed out rather dramatically in a scene involving Paul and a Roman governor named Felix. After nearly being killed in Jerusalem by a band of forty men who plotted his death, Paul was transferred to Caesarea to appear before Felix. Paul's accusers were also ordered to present their case against Paul (Acts 23:12-30). Subsequently, Ananias, the high priest in Jerusalem, went down to Caesarea after Paul had been transferred. Several other high-ranking Jewish leaders joined him. They also took with them a lawyer named Tertullus, who presented their case before Felix. In essence, they accused Paul of being a "troublemaker" wherever he went because of his views regarding Jesus Christ, and they accused him of trying "to desecrate the temple" (24:5-8).

Paul was then given an opportunity to defend himself. He denied the charges, explaining that some Jews in the province of Asia were the ones who really stirred up the people in Jerusalem by making a false charge (21:27-29). At the same time, Paul quickly acknowledged that he followed Jesus Christ and His teachings. "I believe everything that agrees with the Law and that is written in the Prophets," Paul stated, "and I have the same hope in God as these men, that there will be a resurrection of both the righteous and the wicked" (24:14-15).

After hearing Paul's case, Felix dismissed his accusers and ordered Paul be kept under guard but to be given limited freedom. Several days later, he called for Paul. This time, however, he brought along his wife, Drusilla, who was also a Jew. Paul had an opportunity to share with both of them his faith in Jesus Christ.

Luke then records a statement that helps us understand what Paul really meant when he wrote to Titus regarding being disciplined. "As Paul discoursed on righteousness, self-control, and the judgment to come, Felix was afraid and said, 'That's enough for now! You may leave. When I find it convenient, I will send for you'" (24:25).

Self-control is a form of the word Paul used for "discipline" when writing to Titus. What he said convicted Felix to the point that he was gripped with fear.

This reaction tells us a lot about this man's lifestyle. Felix was a typical Roman governor. Though he was evidently a fairly good leader and somewhat partial to the Jews, one reason being that his wife was Jewish, he was in bondage to the desires of the flesh. When Paul shared the Gospel and what it meant to have faith in Jesus Christ, he explained more than just a simple message of easy belief. He put his finger squarely on this man's sin and what God expects from a Christian.

Felix was scared. He knew in his heart what kind of unrighteous and undisciplined person he was, and he feared the future and what would happen when he faced eternity. But like so many people today, he ignored the Holy Spirit's conviction. He wanted religion on his own terms.

Ironically, and in spite of the conviction in his heart, Felix revealed one of his weaknesses. Luke records, "At the same time he was hoping that Paul would offer him a bribe, so he sent for him frequently and talked with him" (24:26). In other words, he was willing to experience some conviction in order to get some money under the table. Not only was he a typical Roman leader in terms of morals, but he was also dishonest and unethical. Political payoffs from the Jews were no doubt common.

I appreciate so much Paul's boldness. He didn't back off from a difficult situation. It's obvious he was tactful in addressing Felix, but he was also straightforward, in spite of the fact that his message of truth may have intensified his own problems. Indeed it did, for Paul was never released by Felix. In fact, two years went by, and eventually Felix was succeeded by Porcius Festus. "But because Felix wanted to grant a favor to the Jews, he left Paul in prison" (24:27). This he did in spite of the fact that there was no solid case against Paul. In this sense he followed in the footsteps of another Roman leader named Pilate who also wanted to please the Jews and turned over an innocent man to be crucified. That man was Jesus Christ.

A New Testament Exhortation

Paul uses a form of the same Greek word in writing to the Corinthians in 1 Corinthians 7. Here he is very specific. He is dealing with sexual behavior. After answering the Corinthians' questions regarding husband-wife relationships by explaining the sanctity of sexual intimacy in marriage (7:1-7), he addresses the questions asked by the unmarried. "Now to the unmarried and the widows I say: it is good for them to stay unmarried, as I am. But if they cannot control themselves, they should marry, for it is better to marry than to burn with passion" (7:8-9).

Here Paul is not teaching that singleness is a better lifestyle in God's sight than marriage. This would be contradictory to the very reason God created Eve—to be a companion for Adam. But there are some people who can serve God better as singles, such as Paul himself. He did not impose his lifestyle on others, and he acknowledged that some people need a marital relationship in order to handle their sexual desires in the will of God. In doing so, he is also teaching that sexual intimacy outside the bonds of marriage is wrong. Furthermore, he is teaching that lack of discipline in this area of our lives is also wrong and sinful. Indeed, this is one of the areas of life where we must exercise self-discipline. For to violate this Law of God, particularly as Christians, leads to serious emotional and spiritual problems.

Never before in the history of our own culture have we ignored God's moral standards as we do today. Premarital sex is no longer thought of as being wrong or sinful by many, many people. Even people who claim to be Christians, and in many instances, who are Christians, have few convictions in this area. The standard is no longer the clear teachings of the Bible; rather the standard is what *we* want. One area of life in which it is especially easy to rationalize our behavior is the area of sexual desire.

In essence, Paul is teaching self-discipline in this area of our lives. This is a major reason why Felix was so uncomfortable. The value system in Rome was totally contradictory to the value system of Christianity, and Paul evidently minced no words with Felix—just as he minces no words in this warning to the Galatians. "Do not be deceived: God cannot be mocked. A man reaps what he sows. The one who sows to please his sinful nature, from that nature will reap destruction; the one who sows to please the Spirit, from the Spirit will reap eternal life" (Gal. 6:7-8).

A New Testament Illustration

Later in 1 Corinthians, Paul uses an illustration from the world of sports to get his point across regarding the importance of self-discipline. "Do you not know that in a race all the runners run, but only one gets the prize? Run in such a way as to get the prize. Everyone who competes in the games goes into strict training" (9:24-25).

In the New International Version, the translators use the phrase *strict training* to translate the same word Paul used earlier to teach discipline in sexual behavior. In this sports illustration, he uses the word to describe the discipline necessary to become a winner.

I remember when my youngest daughter, Robyn, was a student at Baylor University. She got into running and decided to compete in a marathon. To get ready she began a very strict training program, running an average of 6 miles a day and 20 miles every Saturday. She continued this training program for a number of months. I was tremendously impressed with her commitment and self-discipline. It paid off, because she completed her first marathon averaging an 8½ minute mile. Five minutes after running 26 miles, she was breathing normally and experiencing very little physical discomfort. She achieved her personal goal.

Paul goes on to remind the Corinthians that sports enthusiasts go into a strict training program to "get a crown that will not last" (1 Cor. 9:25). And that's not wrong! It must be a thrill to win a Super Bowl ring, and you can see the emotional satisfaction that often overwhelms gold, silver, and bronze medalists as they stand in tiered position receiving their awards at the Olympics. I get choked up with them, especially when they begin playing the national anthem. But most Christians know this is a temporary recognition, "a crown that will not last." Thus Paul reminds the Corinthians that as Christians we should go into strict training to "get a crown that will last forever" (v. 25). If athletes go into strict training to win human rewards, how much more so should Christians go into strict training to receive eternal rewards.

Here Paul is not talking about salvation. He has already made this clear to the Corinthians.

> By the grace God has given me, I laid a foundation as an expert builder, and someone else is building on it. But each one should be careful how he builds. For no one can lay any foundation other than the one already laid, which is Jesus Christ. If any man builds on this foundation using gold, silver, costly stones, wood, hay or straw, his work will be shown for what it is, because the Day will bring it to light. It will be revealed with fire, and the fire will test the quality of each man's work. (3:10-13)

Paul then explains that he is talking not to non-Christians, but to Christians. They will not lose their salvation if they are truly saved. But they may lose their rewards. "If what he has built survives, he will receive his reward. If it is burned up, he will suffer loss; he himself will be saved, but only as one escaping through the flames" (3:14-15).

Paul's Personal Struggle

In 1 Corinthians 9 Paul reminds the Corinthians that they are not alone in their struggle to be self-disciplined. He too faced the same struggles and temptations. Sexual purity, for example, did not just happen for Paul. "Therefore I do not run like a man running aimlessly; I do not fight like a man beating the air. No, I beat my body and make it my slave so that after I have preached to others, I myself will not be disqualified for the prize" (9:26-27).

Unfortunately, some have interpreted Paul's statement that he "beat his body" to justify an ascetic approach to life, particularly involving punishment of the physical body. Paul did not literally beat his body to bring it under control. The essence of Paul's illustration is that as an athlete beats his body with physical training, so must a Christian undergo spiritual training. We'll never overcome temptation and maintain self-discipline without going into strict training spiritually.

Struggles Today

A trend has become evident in our society. We've become preoccupied with sex. Even people who are married have allowed this preoccupation to become an all-absorbing obsession. Eventually it will destroy what God has created to be sacred and satisfying.

Paul must have gotten very specific with Felix and his wife as he discoursed on righteousness and self-discipline—so much so that it made them very uncomfortable. Permit me to be very specific as well. The entertainment industry recently reported that a great percentage of those people today who are renting X-rated videos are married couples who view these explicit materials depicting fornication, adultery, homosexuality, and group sex in the privacy of their own bedrooms. Recently a Christian woman called in to a Christian radio talk show in Dallas and publicly acknowledged that she and her husband rented X-rated videos regularly to stimulate their sex life and saw nothing wrong with it.

There are several things wrong with this behavior. It is spiritually wrong to deliberately watch other people commit sexual sins that are condemned by God, and that is the essence of pornography. People who do so are committing the same sin as those who used to go down to the pagan temples in Ephesus and Corinth to watch live sex orgies. It's the same kind of sin that the people committed who attended the Roman amphitheaters to watch live sex shows. Watching this kind of real-life behavior on film or video is just a more sophisticated way of indulging in sin. It simply captures these sinful actions in permanent form for multiple viewing.

This kind of behavior is also psychologically damaging, and that too is sin, not only against God, but against oneself and one's marital partner. Pornography causes people to set up unrealistic expectations of each other because pornography is based on an unrealistic view of sexual performance. It features a fantasy world. Furthermore, it leads to deterioration, causing people to want more and more explicit and deviant material to create sexual stimulation. It's a never-ending downhill trip to self-destruction.

It's also wrong because it's physically (and psychologically) addictive for many people—particularly men. Frequently this leads the marital partner to forsake the other to view pornography and enter a fantasy world of self-love. When that happens, what God created to be mutually satisfying and rewarding has virtually been destroyed. The capacity for mutual satisfaction is nearly gone.

My heart goes out to young people who are caught in this trap, and many are, even in the preteen years. Before they even marry, they've seen and tried it all. Their relationships are destroyed before they begin. Their potential for happiness together can be destroyed. If the divorce rate is high now—and it is—I predict pornography will multiply this sinful tragedy many times in years to come.

A New Testament Application

As we conclude, let's go back to the story of Paul and Felix. Why was this Roman governor so uncomfortable with Paul's discourse on "righteousness, self-control and the judgment to come"? The answer is obvious. God's standard cut across this man's lifestyle. Paul put his finger on his problem. He was not living a righteous life nor was he living a disciplined life.

What About You?

Does the Word of God make you feel uncomfortable? Do you want to say, "That's enough for now! I want out of here. When I find it convenient, I'll be back."

At the same time, maybe you have ambivalent feelings that bring you back, perhaps because it is profitable to be in church. After all, people in our culture still like to do business with churchgoers. There are lots of good contacts in the religious community. In short, I think God—through this New Testament situation involving Governor Felix—is asking all of us what our motives are for going to church.

Perhaps you're like Felix and his wife, Drusilla. You are "well acquainted with the Way" (Acts 24:22). But you've never come to know Jesus Christ personally, who said, "I am the way and the truth and the life. No man comes to the Father but by Me" (John 14:6). May I plead with you *not* to respond like this Roman couple? Accept Jesus Christ now. As we read in Hebrews, "Today, if you hear His voice, do not harden your hearts" (Heb. 3:15; 4:7). And John wrote, "He came to that which was His own, but His own [the Jews] did to receive Him. Yet to all who received Him, to those who believed in His name, He gave the right to become children of God" (John 1:11-12).

Have you received Jesus Christ personally? You can, by simply and sincerely asking Christ to be your personal Saviour. This prayer may help you.

Father, I confess to You I have failed You in various ways, and I acknowledge that as sin.

Dear God, thank You for sending Your Son to die for

my sins and to rise again from the dead so that I might have eternal life.

Dear Jesus, I now invite You to be my personal Saviour from sin. Come into my life and make me Your very own.

Thank You, dear Lord, for giving me eternal life. Thank You for the Holy Spirit who now dwells in my life.

I pray that I might always live so as to please You. In Jesus' name. Amen.

Have you decided to follow Jesus Christ and His way of life? Perhaps you are a Christian. You're struggling with discipline in some area of your life. You're struggling with the discipline involved in making a decision to do what you know is right. Without making that decision and reinforcing it with truth, you will never change your attitudes and actions. Will you make that decision today? This prayer may help you.

Dear Father, I here and now decide to follow Your will and desires rather than my will and desires. Help me to act on that decision, with Your help to eliminate in my life those things that displease You, with Your help to be obedient to the Word of God, with Your help to do everything I can to reinforce this decision so that I don't slip back into my old habits. These things I pray in Jesus' name. Amen.

A FINAL WORD

Do you want people to like and respect you God's way? In essence, this is what the Bible means by having a good reputation. Paul teaches that a mature Christian will "have a good reputation with outsiders" as well as with fellow Christians. And then Paul states why this is important—so we won't "fall into disgrace and into the devil's trap" (1 Tim. 3:7). There are people who dislike Christians, and they always will. But we should never be guilty of being disliked and not respected because we have violated God's principles of Christlike living.

Check yourself. To what extent are you reflecting these qualities to others—in your family, in your church, and in the world? Are you overbearing, quick-tempered, overindulgent, violent, or dishonest? Or do you show hospitality, love what is good, exercise self-control, act uprightly, live in a holy manner, and exercise discipline?

Discover your areas of strength and weakness. Thank God for your strengths and then set up goals to overcome your weaknesses. Outline specific steps you're going to take to achieve these goals. You may find these suggestions helpful

144 / God's Plan for Building a Good Reputation

as you work on your weaker areas.

- Share your need with a close and trusted friend—perhaps your mate. Ask that person to pray for you and with you.
- Pray every day for strength to overcome your weaknesses and to reach your goals.
- Memorize Scripture verses that will help you overcome your weaknesses. Go back through the chapters to find some of these verses and use a concordance to find additional ones.
- Ask people you've hurt in areas where you have failed to reflect these qualities to forgive you. If these people are Christians, ask them for their personal prayer support as you develop positive qualities in your life.

DATE DUE